by Tom Clark

Airplanes (1966)

The Sandburg (1966)

Emperor of the Animals (1967)

Stones (1969)

Air (1970)

Neil Young (1971)

The No Book (1971)

Green (1971)

Smack (1972)

John's Heart (1972)

Blue (1974)

At Malibu (1975)

Fan Poems (1976)

Baseball (1976)

Champagne and Baloney (1976)

35 (1976)

No Big Deal (1977)

How I Broke In (1977)

The Mutabilitie of the Englishe Lyrick (1978)

When Things Get Tough on Easy Street: Selected Poems 1963–1978 (1978)

The World of Damon Runyon (1978)

One Last Round for the Shuffler (1979)

Who Is Sylvia? (1979)

The Great Naropa Poetry Wars (1980)

The Last Gas Station and Other Stories (1980)

The End of the Line (1980)

A Short Guide to the High Plains (1981)

Heartbreak Hotel (1981)

Nine Songs (1981)

Under the Fortune Palms (1982)

Jack Kerouac (1984)

Paradise Resisted: Selected Poems 1978–1984 (1984)

Property (1984)

The Border (1985)

Late Returns: A Memoir of Ted Berrigan (1985)

His Supposition (1986)

The Exile of Céline (1987)

Disordered Ideas (1987)

Apocalyptic Talkshow (1987)

Easter Sunday (1988)

The Poetry Beat: Reviewing the Eighties (1990)

Fractured Karma (1990)

Charles Olson: The Allegory of a Poet's Life (1991)

Sleepwalker's Fate: New and Selected Poems 1965–1991 (1992)

Robert Creeley and the Genius of the American Common Place (1993)

Junkets on a Sad Planet: Scenes from the Life of John Keats (1994)

Like Real People (1995)

Empire of Skin (1997)

TOM CLARK

EMPIRE OF SKIN

PREFACE BY EDWARD DORN

BLACK SPARROW PRESS
SANTA ROSA 1997

ACKNOWLEDGMENTS

Some of these poems first appeared in *Exquisite Corpse, Gas, Mike and Dale's Younger Poets* and *Yale Younger Poets.*

Cover art: View of the entrance of Nootka Sound at a distance of three leagues.

Black Sparrow Press books are printed on acid-free paper.

LIBRARY OF CONGRESS CATALOGING-IN-PUBLICATION DATA

Clark, Tom, 1941–
    Empire of skin / Tom Clark.
      p.   cm.
    ISBN 1-57423-049-2 (pbk. : alk. paper). — ISBN 1-57423-050-6 (cloth trade : alk. paper). — ISBN 1-57423-051-4 (signed cloth : alk. paper)
    I. Title.
PS3553.L29E47   1997
811'.54—dc21
                                           97-37463
                                              CIP

homing bird

Tom Clark

TABLE OF CONTENTS

PART TWO: ADVENTURES IN THE SKIN TRADE

1. EXTRICATION

2. CONTACT

3. THE RACE BEGINS

4. SPHERES OF INTEREST

5. AMONG THE AMERICANS

6. THREE EMPIRES

7. HARD BARGAIN

8. CAPTIVE

Preface

In the American westward expansion from the Atlantic coastal ranges to the Pribilof Islands, the search for peltry led the way before all other exploitation—mining, ranching, land hunger and manifested psychopolitical space. The hunter and trapper followed the streams and trails of fur bearers across the continents and around the Horn into the greatest hoard of fur ever known—the "soft gold" of this account—the Pacific Northwest, where European empires met to capture the trade in pelts, and for those with a mission for it, the harvest of some of the most savage souls ever encountered on this globe.

But such interesting madness has long since degenerated into the breathless venalities of real-estate. The great Northwest has seen the banning of the Potlatch and the chain reaction elevation of the Kaffeeklatsch, with the economic depredations of its habits far removed to the peonage of Central and South America. And of course the richest man in the world is not a buccaneer capitalist underwriting the explorations of a Captain Cook, but is yet a son of the Puget Sound, whose skin looks as thin as a microchip.

The Pacific Northwest was the last of the late 18th and 19th century frontiers (for both Russians and Americans) and it is still "the last frontier," a catch phrase which is the motto of Alaska. *Empire of Skin* is the recapitulation of the greatest hunting enterprise of the millennium, which brought the grounding and mapping of what is now demarked by the geo-commercial term "Pacific Rim." The story encompasses the somber pursuit of prolific creatures whose evolution made them irresistible to a race born without the hats and coats necessary for surviving extreme latitudes. This was the last great raid on nature before 19th century chemistry began to break out the chains of synthetics, allowing the masses a measure of warmth and affording the comfortable, morally opportunistic condemnation of the wearing of animal fur.

This is a beautifully founded document. This book is created with a poetry which carries the authority of the full modern tradition. Its exactitudes of diction generate and inform the imagination. And finally it is only poetry that is capable of saving such extensive cultural memory from the decaying vortex of history.

Ed Dorn, Denver, 1997

Empire of Skin

Part One: Apparitional Canoe

apparitional canoe

a singing   wind rushed

                   through cedars

       silver moonlit

    beached whale   gleamed

out on the Sound

          wave washed

otters slept on kelp beds

       back-floating

mild

They're easy together
                    inside the pod
when there's no hunting

the yelp of the little
one is not heard   on good days

when the weather is mild they move

      like the vowels in the word
                        repose

off shore to browse
            among sea
                        urchin and mussel
                  encrusted submerged reefs

or in drifting patches of
                  floating kelp

swimming on her back

swimming on her back
   protecting a sleeping
     pup on her chest
a mother moves hurriedly
and steadily on the surface
from where the rising wind
is causing rough water
to where it isn't doing this
while over at the other
edge of the pack   a male
after emerging with a fish
        from a food dive
is swimming on his back
consuming the fish   in
a few minutes he moves
to another spot   still eating
        his departure
prompted by the presence
of three glaucous winged
             gulls
flying above him nervous
mockingly picking up
his discarded food scraps

lotus

That great growing natural
       mattress—sleeping
place and feeding ground
can be your undoing
          A stranded otter
sleeping on a kelp bed
afternoon siesta extends into
unintentional ride on a large
free-floating kelp raft
headed to an offshore island
      watchful hunters around
tides move sleeping animals farther
            & farther out
to deeper water beyond
feeding area—you seem breathless
returning from this long
  snooze on duty

       kelp ride nap
carried you into killing
      ground

the hunt

I've looked over the hunter's shoulder
seen the otter grab her pup and dive
        down into her world
the plunging spills still water aside
        bubbles   aeration   body's
reverberation washing through the mid-deep
                             green
under
     world   stirred   fur
light flashing amidst plankton   air
    pockets   sleeked back   flippers
hydro
      planing

I've seen the chase—
some pursue   some celebrate
                       the fortune
                         of the hunt

But I've seen too
escape dives of long duration through
a world of krill

       the female's   capable
       heart aflutter   blood pumping

    to elude the thrashing kill

dream of otter's swimming down & away song

In escape dive pursued
    fifty-one minutes by intent
humans   make a one
half meter under water
            quick
full turn to
escape a dip net dead ahead
and roll off left
        and down a stair
case
     submerged ocean ridges
into twenty fathom water

stay down
      six minutes

up at the surface   none too soon
see the craft turn
back   then hear
the pup squeal
      and come up
into the eye of the harpoon

captivity

matted with filth
soaked to the skin
stiff with cold   rigid
my waterproofing
destroyed once
I am returned to
cold water
I will chill & die
knowing this
I attempt to escape
tearing at the wire
screen cage
with my teeth & forepaws

old days

old days used to be
one on one hunting
hunter and steersman get up
go out to kelp beds
before daybreak fine morning
come up silent running
soundless in polished hull
canoe rolling on small swell
otter catching forty winks
wakened by the arrow

night hunt

calm night moonlight in cedars
a little soft wind a cloud or
two blowing over glassy water
go out along reefs in a
polished-hull ottering canoe
sit tight wait till mother hunting
leaves pup alone one time
paddle toward sound of pup crying
pup's easy to grab tie a rope
around its neck toss it back
in the water make it swim around
poke it a little scared squealing
alert mother worried comes
up from food dive to investigate
get in your best shot she'll still fight
gasping and tearing at the barb
trying to bite off the point

mass hunt for trade—1

you don't want to make any noise
in the water that is going to
wake up and scare off a snoozing otter
you want your canoe hull to be glassy smooth
you polish it till you can see your face
carry it like a baby down to the water
the chief who owns the water speaks
the hunters line up their canoes
the killing line forms outside the breakers
the hunt director's raised-paddle signals
outlined against the Sound in
quickly breaking morning light
draw the canoes in a closing arc
around the first otter sighted
the hunters sit tense arrows to strings
the otter comes up on a swell
surfacing from a deep escape dive
the noose of the canoe line closes
the first twangs of the bows
echo over the quiet water

mass hunt for trade—2

when the otter comes up
    bobbing on kelp winded
the steersman rolls
    his polished hull on the swell
holding the canoe steady
    the arrows fly in volleys
the metal points have reversed barbs
    don't drive deep but stick fast
identifying the lucky hitter
    marking the catch as his
the hunters close in for the kill
    the fortunate first marksman's
steerer stands up in his rolling
    canoe and yells out in triumph
announcing the pay in wealth goods
    to be shared out to other shooters
who drive home successive hits
    blood pours out on the water

after the hunt

the hunters paddle back
to the village
with the happy steersmen
out front loudly
announcing who's had hits
and who's had kills

some ritual business at the lake

There was a lake out by
      the winter village
where the sea otter hunter went to
      take care of business

He made 200 bunches
      of needly hemlock branches
and racked them up
      on some fish-drying poles

He went out there and sang
      and scoured himself
till there were no needles left
      on any hemlock branch

He waded out chest deep
      and hunkered down
and duckwalked all around
      the shoreline of the lake

Every now and then
      he sucked in a big breath
and dunked himself all the way
      down into the cold water

That's what a sea otter
      on the run from
a hunter in a canoe
      has to do

This happened just before
    the Elder Moon
and after he was done
      the man went sea otter hunting

the whaler's wife

The whaler's wife represents the whale
she has to cover her bed
with brand new mats
and lie quiet while
the hunt's going on
to keep the whale from
            getting too restless

A slug placed on top of the mats
will go in the direction
in which the whale
            will turn

Whales are attracted
            to whalers' wives
            and to fresh water
whale towing chants
address the towed whale
as 'Chief's wife'
or 'Queen'

Whales aren't easy to tow
you can try offering the whale
            a drink of fresh water
one Ahousat towing
            song goes

'Take it easy, Queen'

lost souls

sometimes out in the woods
you'll run into *puqmis*
lost human souls
see them just before
you become one of them
say you're out hunting
your canoe gets tipped over
you get yourself ashore somehow
you're standing there shivering
that's when the *puqmis* pops out
ugly white skin like an albino
awful bulging eyes
woos you back into the woods
makes you think you can get yourself warm
at his cabin
runs along so fast leading you there
on his long claws
you can't keep up

solitary loon

Narrow valleys, steep hills, bare, stony or snow-dusted peaks, shining rain pools, long, thin, tarn-like lochs extending withered fingers for miles in notches between pine-fledged mountain ridges. Silence but for the melancholy cry of the loon, the breaking of a decayed branch in the woods, the bubbling rush of the torrent.

in the woods

A right hand sticking out of the ground
holds a rattle and shakes it
a left hand sticking out of the ground
—don't look!

Mallards with no heads have
brilliant plumage but don't fly
birds with human faces
should never be looked at
mountain lions walking backward
kill people with their tails

The souls of trees
are shadowy things
that quickly step out from behind trees
and then quickly step back
—shut your eyes!

Gartersnakes
zip out of their dens
at the speed of light
and throw themselves
little devil darts
into every orifice of
your horrified body

Dwarves have houses inside mountains
they invite you to dance with them
around a big wooden drum
you get dizzy and trip over the drum

pretty soon you come down with
a terrible case of trembling foot

Stones in the woods sometimes turn into mirrors
when you see yourself in them
blood begins pouring out of your mouth also
simultaneously out of your sinus cavity

Shaman squirrels run around in the woods
watch out for them
they sing and shake tiny rattles
they like to do this over old rotten logs
their songs are so strong
the logs start to tremble and groan

primeval interior

The land is choked with
    biomass both
dead and living   up
    from the dank lush moss rug
underfoot   through trunks of
    fallen trees strewn
across every foot path   to
    lichen dangling   thin white
old lace   from ancient
    limbs

Things Happening in the Sky

i. eclipse

When the sky codfish
swallows up the sun
or the moon, it's real
trouble. That's why
people sing songs and
pound on planks to scare
the sky codfish away.

ii. snow

When the sky dog,
a big mangy cur
who lives way up in
the air, scratches
his mange sores,
the scales fall away
and flutter down
to earth. That's why
children shouldn't eat snow.

iii. fog

The supernatural crane
releases fog from
his kneecaps   no wonder
the feathered serpent—
the dog of the thunder
bird—hides his lightning
(the flapping of his wings)
under a rotten log

ritual business

i.

Really big sharks
live in deep holes
at the foot of steep cliffs
can swallow an entire canoe
in one bite—why war chiefs
who want to get really tough
pick those spots to do
their bathing rituals

ii.

At his bathing place
he prepares his twig bundles
a sentry box with spook paintings
his shrine contains
masks and skulls maybe
empty eyesocket
desiccated corpse

Once at Ahousat
a wolf walked into
somebody's whaling shrine

Wolves are pretty strong but
that wolf dropped dead
                on the spot

iii.

A man was found dead
one morning

at his bathing place
he'd stayed out
all night long
immersed in that
very cold water
scrubbing himself with
thick bundles of nettles
rubbing up against some
barnacle-covered rocks
and dragging his body over
some small jagged shells

a supernatural
creature must have got him

the ya'ai

The *ya'ai* look like men
except for the tufts of feathers

that grow out of their ears
they come paddling right up to you

in a supernatural canoe
their bodies are white and hairy

I am killing whales
because I got made strong

by the ten *ya'ai*
who stand outside my door

at the midwinter shaman's dance

The men who led the songs were dressed
    in black blankets

These were the men I dreamed

When they came in everybody got serious
    all the laughing stopped

During the songs
    some men drummed accompaniment

All the people in the house sang

After four songs had been sung
    the speaker said 'Quiet!'

Not a sound could be heard above
    the wind soughing in the trees
    the wind whistling in the trees

    the water lapping on the beach
    the water washing on the beach

The speaker then stepped forward and said
    the singing had been in vain
    the Wolves had not heard it
    the Supernatural Wolves

The song leaders took off the ceremonial outfits
        the audience shouted a lot of abuse at them
And then the speaker stepped forward and said
        'We need a new song leader'

like jungle book

fables of northern
nature kingdoms
pristine creation
a frozen dream

like jungle book on ice
hunters moving across
the land bridge through
the Straits down into

America   meeting
more hunters coming
Indians Russians bringing
original sin

vodka fish
hooks chisels
billy clubs
guns

the proschylenniks

The *proschylenniks*
   come out of
Kamchatka
   endarkened
by Okhotsk
   vodka get
skins to take
   back east
from Irkutsk
   pink fog of blood
before long
   otters are gone
hunters move on
   at traders' will
a tracer imbedded
   in the fleeing pods
pursued from rivermouth
   ice floe to ice
floe south until
   meeting up in
some warmer inlet
   with the canoe
making killers
   coming up
north through
   offshore kelp
beds with harpoons
   and muskets

before contact

                Indian wars and yet
peace in every upstream elbow of the inlet

In early summer the sea is glassy calm
fog banks form on the margin of
the Japan current, out offshore, where
                     sea otters swim,
and roll in day after day, morning
               after morning,
breaking up only when a slight
           breeze rises

the evil star dawning
              with the white
sail on the horizon

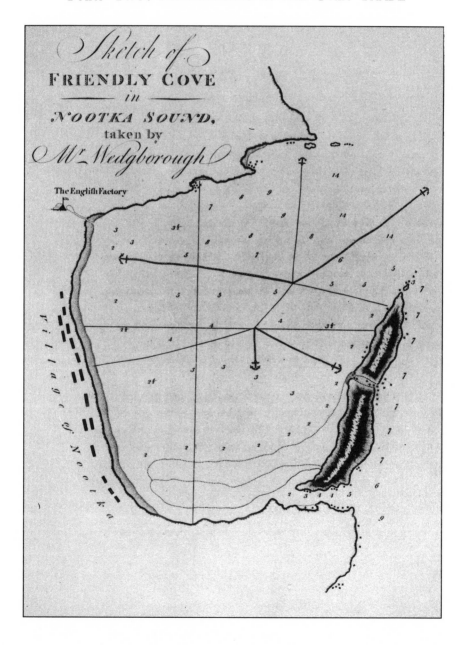

Sketch of
FRIENDLY COVE
in
NOOTKA SOUND,
taken by
Mr Wedgborough

The English Factory

1
Extrication

The Agreement of Nature & Trade
(the chimney sweeper's cry)

The earth was made for ——————— to trade
in, and the sun and moon were made to give them
light. Rivers and seas were formed to float their
ships; rainbows gave them promise of fair weather;
winds blew for or against their enterprises; stars and
planets circled in their orbits, to preserve inviolate a
system of which they were the center.

extrication

failing the rescue by legacy

entailment

or sudden settlement

emigration——

go out on a ship

the vacuum   allows

of penetration

50

the threat to quality

Fanny Burney's brother was a Navy Man
Burney
Dixon, Portlock, Colnett, Vancouver—all
sailed under Cook

'This City is so filled with Workmen, dust, & lime, that you really want two pair of Eyes to walk about in it,—one for being put out, & the other to see with afterwards.'

F.B. 8 September, 1791 (Bath)

The fall from grace is cruel   Meares aboard
the threat to quality   the *Nootka* stuck
lose your fortune   out on the ice
get out of the way   of Unalaska
don't embarrass your   with two Lascars
friends by staying   and a large New-
escape route for the debt   foundland dog named
haunted & ruined   Towser, all winter '86–'87
—'trade'   against a hostile
          'America'   Indian nation

Voyages autour du Monde
(Cook and the Burneys)

Capt. Cook came to dinner at Queen Square
high excitement should brother Jem
get to sail under the great navigator
go out into Empire   Miss B.
thought the great navigator a dunce
on any subject but his own great purpose
('apparently under a pressure of mental
fatigue when called upon to speak,
or stimulated to deliberate, upon
any other')   Cook drew tracks over
Bougainville's charts for Jem
Voyages autour du Monde
'and made some curious remarks
on the illiberal conduct of that
circum-navigator towards himself'
The family preserved Cook's pencil
scribbles under skin-milk fixative
'There is talk of his intended expedition'
Jem sailed round the world with him
learned reefs and leeshores scurvy
and cannibals could kill got skins
at Nootka sailed for China saw
Cook sent to the savage shades of Owyhee
              survived
'the tragical history of blood'
vision of the sacrificial pyre flickering
         through palm fronds
to bring *Discovery* home
out of Empire

                              —and
'wretched weather, much
danger, infinite sickness,
& no prize!'
                    —Fanny, 1780

gaslight

Great flower that opens at night
      huge gaseous bilious
City of business of ships Cook
      not fated to come home to

London by gaslight
more lamps in the Oxford
road alone than in all Paris
the great world metropolis mapped
      out in fire

The iron lilies of the Strand
      shone down on the press gangs

a sudden beaming eye in
whose sight dreams of capital
      grow visible
      and bright

The Skin Game (Old World)

'The pestilent lanes and alleys which, in their vocabulary, go by the names of Rotten-Row, Gibraltar-place, and Booble-alley, are putrid with vice and crime; to which, perhaps, the round globe does not offer a parallel. The sooty and begrimed bricks of the very houses have a reeking, Sodom-like, and murderous look; and well may the shroud of coal-smoke, which hangs over this part of the town, more than any other, attempt to hide the enormities there practiced. These are the haunts from which sailors sometimes disappear for ever; or issue in the morning, robbed naked, from the broken doorways.'

—Melville, *Redburn*

the threat to quality—2

foot pad—see low pad. Generally a bloody and
merciless crew of villains.
A New Canting Dict., 1725

ANDREW BAYNES, A FOOTPAD (a micrological elegy)

This Andrew Baynes was from his infancy of a vicious
inclination, and though he had the natural sense to know
he was in an error, yet he was resolved his heart should
still be the same. When he first displayed his vanity he
began with defrauding and cheating all he had to deal
with, especially by taking great houses and then getting
upholsterers to furnish 'em, ran away with their goods at
night. Thus would he also treat braziers, pewterers,
limners, cabinet-makers, and other tradesmen, as partic-
ularly once by taking a house in Red Lion Square, from
whence he carried out about £400 worth of goods into the
Mint, but was took out from thence by a *Posse Comitatus*
and sent to gaol.

Being unsuccessful in housebreaking, he resolved to
try his fortune in turning footpad, which is the high-road
to Hell.

This malefactor, executed at Tyburn in 1711, aged 26
years, was born in Essex and last served as a drawer at
the Blue Posts Tavern at the corner of Portugal Street by
Lincoln's Inn back-gate. He was very undutiful to his an-
cient mother who went a-begging; and the woman he
kept company with was called Flum, for her formerly
selling Flummery, being the leavings of one George Pur-
chase, a bailiff condemned (but reprieved) for high trea-
son with one Damary, a waterman, for the insurrection

made by the rabble in London when Dr. Henry Sacheverall was tried by the Peers upon several articles exhibited against him by the House of Commons.

skin the lamb

1811 *Lex. Bal.* Frisk the skin of the stephen; empty the money out of the purse.

USA A fur. Pejorative; ex trappers'. 1920 On the skin, engaged in fur stealing.

1753 John Poulter, *Discoveries.* He went and skin'd the Trunk, and put the Things into a sack.

1812 J. H. Vaux. To strip a man of all his money at play, is termed *skinning* him.

The skin game. Swindling, esp. card-sharping and confidence-trickery.

1797 Potter. Skinners, kidnappers, or set of abandoned fellows who steal children, or intrap unwary men to inlist for soldiers.

Skin-merchant. A recruiting officer. 1781 Burgoyne, *Lord of the Manor.* I am a manufacturer of honor and glory—vulgarly called a recruiting dealer—or, more vulgarly still, a skin merchant.

extrication—2

young men denied
settlement must go
out into   Empire

ordinary   or officers
seamen   thrown in with

former
footpads   pressed
        by gangs
from pubs
inns   or prison ships

Exchange Society (the skin trade)

proposes property as human quality
                               to be dealt in
a vicious circle of representations
                    and accommodations
between intensity and social settlement
until (finally) one can't continue
                    to keep up the game

resignation, then, remains
that and/or extrication

like John McKay, left   a single person going off on his own
behind for the winter   had better learn through distancing,
at Indian village—   once having come up lame,
turned 'wild'   what history couldn't teach him—
the hard way   struggling to break free of the game,

a dutifully sustained
                    external complication

60

Portlock took

Nathaniel   midshipman
Portlock   1785–1786   under Cook
            to Nootka with the *King George*

Portlock took
persons of place

sons of Regency
gentlemen to school

in wild and pathless seas
the Empire

universally available
escape route

black sheep
could be lost in it

ruined or misunderstood
heroic youth

the weak of every kind
transferred to it

2
CONTACT

In the Sound the apparitional canoe
sailing upriver (the inlet) evening

After supper didn't come below
again until well past eight
the faint steady breeze
was loaded with dew the
wet darkened sails held all there
was of propelling power in it
the night clear and starry
sparkled darkly the opaque
lightless patches shifting slowly
against the low stars were
the drifting islets on the
port bow there was a bigger island
more distant and shadowily
imposing by the great space
of sky it eclipsed closed
my eyes and time passed
opened my eyes a second time started
my heart with a thump a great fjord
seemed to hang right over the ship
mass of blackness there was not a
gleam to be seen not a sound

landfall

The first thing the sailing man
from the old world saw   after nearly going
fathoms down on unseen offshore
reefs underwater ocean ridges outlying
were rocks and shingle beaches
long Pacific rollers broke and roared
peaks clad with dark spruce and fir
and crowned with snow rose
to clouds which distilled sea borne
moisture down in showers day long
behind the outer margin
of beach the undergrowth spread
dank and impenetrable
as a native mind

In the Name of His Imperial Catholic Majesty

To map is not yet
to appropriate (possess)

Natives greeted voyagers with fresh fish
as if experienced at such businesses
      hardly standoffish

1774 Pérez cautious would
      go no further north
into the lavender Arctic twilight
Martínez the Sevillano piloting   the waves
                        sang

Wind rushed in the pines
the Haida circled the *Santiago*
threw feathers on the water
      round the ship   singing
brought sea otter skins as 'gifts'

The drumming of the natives on wooden
planks rang out like unison
volleys of musket fire

Before the trade ships arrived with
conceptual synthesis (wealth goods)
none of this was yet 'history'

the watchman

The Indian sentinel
at Point Lookout—
in pines, the wind rush—
saw white sails
—apparition
of a supernatural creature?
a great horizonal canoe
was rocked like a skiff

the wave wash
pushed its sound back
through the whisper
of wind in the trees

as the canoe was beached

('history' begins with this)

The Commodore (Capt. James Cook)

Cook didn't care about trade
looked to discover
Empire took Cook to Nootka o'er
'pathless and wild seas'

a coasting master
brought techno-nautical
clockwork reckoning
accurate landfall and

some green glass beads
fired at Murano
under water
and by sailor's stars

came away with
sea otter skins
cutsarks as 'gifts'
off Indians' backs

his men slept in that
rich black dense
verminous pelage
all the way back

across the killer ocean
misnamed 'Pacific'
with its chain of gorgeous
murderous paradises

four years later

Cook was shown a silver spoon
stolen from a Spanish ship
                how was it
Resolution and *Discovery*
had been preceded in Exploration?

The spoon had belonged to don Estéban
José Martínez
                the Sevillano
returned in 1789 to Nootka
under agency of Empire
commanding the *Princesa*
natives chanted his name
                pure protocol but
once the singing was done
chiefs kept their silent counsel
    Maquina and Kelekum
outside the ceremonial house
                the wind rushed

Maquina Greeting Cook at Friendly Cove
(Nootka Sound, 1778)

A canoe remarkable for a
   singular head which
      had a bird's eye and a bill

of an enormous size
   painted on it
      a person who was in the bow

seemed to be a chief
   many feathers hanging from his head
      his face painted in extraordinary manner

Maquina greeting Cook
   from the biggest and last in line
      of the Nootkan dugouts

stood up strewing handfuls of
   feathers over the water
      towards us on the ship

as some of his fellow
   Indians threw red dust
      or powder likewise

and made a long harangue
   holding in his hand a carved bird
      of wood

as large as a pigeon
        which he rattled and was
            no less vociferous in his harangue

two or three other natives likewise
        had their hair
            quite strewed over

with small feathers
        others with large ones stuck
            into different parts of their heads

they made a tumultuous
        noise and when this
            noise at length had ceased

they sat in their canoes
        a little distance from the ship
            and conversed with each other

in an easy manner
        some one or other now
            and then getting up

and saying something
        after the manner of
            their first harangues

and one sang a very agreeable air
        with a degree of softness and melody
            we could not have expected

the word *haela* friend
        being often repeated
            as the burden of the song

Local Monopoly
(Cook at Nootka, April 1778)

i.

natives daily visited us
they paddled round both ships
a chief standing up
in canoe spear in hand
most vociferously bawling orator
face sometimes masked
ceremonious circuit round ship
then came alongside
entertained us with a song
their whole company joined in
most agreeable harmony
and then began to traffic

ii.

rival Indians arrived
adverse party in dispute to be adjusted
canoes back and forth
we were probably occasion of the quarrel

strangers insisting on having
a right of sharing
advantages of trade with us
our old friends would not suffer it

evident indeed they engrossed us
entirely to themselves
and carried on a traffic with
more distant tribes

disappeared
four or five days
returned with fresh
cargoes of curiosities and skins

When Wickaninish shows up, Maquina barges in to take his cut (April 21, 1778)

Strangers visited   twelve or thirteen canoes
from the southward Wickaninish
                    and the Clayoquots

turned the point of the Cove
and drew up in a body
two hundred yards from the ships
preparing their ceremony

they advanced standing in their canoes singing
some slow and solemn songs   others in quicker time
with hand motions   paddles beating
                    in concert on the sides

a kind of chorus
the most expressive gestures
then came nearer the ship
and bartered with us for skins

some of our old friends
got in between us and the strangers
and managed the traffic

from the ship's journal

Intending to put to sea
the Captains Cook and Clerke
went with two boats to the village
where Capt. Cook had observed
plenty of grass to get
a supply of this for the goats
and sheep on board
experienced the usual welcome reception
the Commodore ordered his people
to begin cutting not imagining
the natives would object
our furnishing ourselves with
what could not be of any use to them
as soon as our men began cutting grass
some of the inhabitants would not permit
them to proceed   saying '*makook*'
which signified we must buy it first

Brass (Cook at Nootka)

metal was especially demanded
particularly brass with such eagerness
before we left hardly a bit
of it was to be found in the ships
even officers' jackets without buttons

infestation of the merchandise

'one could say that in taking on a cargo of furs
one takes on also a cargo of lice'
              —*Marchand, 1790*

Particularly in the early years when
to get their hands on a few novel articles
of trade the chiefs were willing
to strip the sea otter cloaks
from their own backs and as Cook
says thereby reduce themselves to a state of nudity
many if not most of the skins exchanged
were—Cook again—'very lousy'

inconvenience ashore

'Words can scarcely Convey to the mind of the reader, an adequate idea of the Beastly filth in which the Natives of this part of the world pass their lives; I declare, that before I was an Eye Witness to it, I had a very imperfect conception of the extent of it. It was impossible to move a Single step, without being up to the ankles in Mud, Fish, Guts & Maggots, and this inconvenience was alike felt within and without doors.'

—James Charles Stewart Strange

grooming

sea otters endlessly
grooming 'compusively'
clean

for cold water
survival—air pockets
in pelage

Bell, of Vancouver's party, on the Nootkans:

'extremely filthy and dirty in their persons, dwellings, manner of living and in short in everything whatever ...They seldom or ever wash themselves, and they beautify themselves highly in their opinions by besmearing their faces with Red Ochre and white paint mixed with Fish Oil, in different figures, which at times makes their appearance frightful....

'the combs the women make use of are only for the purpose of combing the Hair smooth and straight and not for destroying vermin...These they conceive too precious to run the risk of losing by using small combs therefore they pick them out with their fingers from each others heads and not willing to go unre-warded for their pains—eat them.'

Cook's report

'The fur of these animals, as mentioned in the Russian accounts, is certainly softer and finer than that of any others we know of and, therefore, the discovery of this part of the continent of North America where so valuable an article of commerce may be met with, cannot be a matter of indifference. There is not the least doubt, that a very beneficial fur trade may be carried on with the inhabitants of this vast coast. But unless a northern passage should be found practicable, it seems rather too remote from Great Britain to receive any emolument from it.'

Meares' Account of the Trade (late 1780s)

Till then the long overland trek toting skins of sea
otters killed by Russian hunters in Kamchatka to
Kiakhta on the Chinese frontier, to exchange for
nankeens and tea to be returned overland to Europe,
made the price three times greater at Kiakhta than at
Okhotsk.

'furs form the principal and favorite dress
of the inhabitants of the Northern provinces of China
and those of the rarest kind and the highest prices
are eagerly purchased by them

from five hundred to one thousand dollars
and even larger sums
are frequently paid for a single
suit of this precious clothing'

a *cutsark* as the mariners called it

haggling with the hong

Capts. Gore and King with Cook's ships
obtained a permit
to trade upriver to Canton
King carried 20 skins in a pinnace

hong offered merchandise
willowware and tea King
demanded Spanish
gold dollars

in the end the parties
split the difference
minimalization
of the cultural divide

Old Canton

Fresh from the savage wilderness how strange
Old Canton! The terraced hongs
With their great go-downs out in front
Screening foreign-devil eyes from the Forbidden City,
Before which flows the Pearl River, bearing dreams!

Mandarin boats move up and down the river slowly
Barging into vision with gay pennants flying,
Propelled by double banks of oars
Moving up and down in hypnotic, stately cadence,
Like pagodas sailing into a busy paradise.

Great tea-deckers, topsides brightly lacquered yellow
        and red,
Squares of brown matting rigged out for sails,
Hauling Souchong, young Hyson and Bohea,
Pass down the aisle of darting sampans,
Each one housing an entire family of floating
        tradespeople.

Twilight falls, as clouds of red and orange spill across the
        sky,
Driving the boat people to their moorings,
A simple bamboo pole thrust in the oozy bottom.
Paper lanterns diffuse a soft glow over the river,
Blunt prows of opium skiffs begin to bump against the
        ship's sides.

The Discovery of Soft Gold
(coming home from Cook's 3rd voyage)

King:
'The rage with which our seamen were possessed to return to Cook's River, and, by another cargo of skins, to make their fortunes, at one time, was not far short of mutiny'

Washington Irving:
'It was as if a new gold coast had been discovered'

Skin Prices: Cook's people
(per piece)

Meanwhile in Macao
private industry
took its course   otter skin
cutsarks some
seamen had slept on
since Nootka
'prime' skins smoky
or sooty in color
$100 to $300

a forward youth

John Ledyard
a Dartmouth lad
ran off with Cook's marines

round the world
on the great adventure
then spent

the rest of his days chasing
a grail of skin
trade prospects

'the greatest commercial
enterprise that has ever been
embarked on in this country'

Jefferson received him in France
John Paul Jones advanced him money
Jefferson 'proposed to him to go

by land to Kamchatka
cross in some Russian vessel
to Nootka Sound fall down

into the latitude of Missouri
and penetrate to and through that to
the United States'

but was (harsh fate) jailed by the Czar
and died at Cairo just about the time
Dixon was bringing home the first great strike

journals of James Burney

Furneaux sent out the cutter for greens
to a bay across the Sound
and when the cutter did not come back
sent Burney in the launch
this was the place Cook
called Grass Cove
Burney found at a small beach
some baskets of
barbequed human tissue
some scraps of clothes
several scattered shoes
two hands
and the head
of a black deckhand
chased the savages
back to Grass Cove
with musket volleys
found the party
still going on over
the cooking stove
'such a shocking scene
of Carnage & Barbarity
as can never be mentioned
or thought of, but
with horror'

second skins

the underdressed celebrants
flaying and filleting it
       for dinner—
the clothing on the ground
around the barbeque pit
    in the frozen wilderness
of Goya's *Cannibals Preparing*
    Their Victims
           shows that
the meat is modern European
    for a civilized traveler
inconvenient being eaten
                one
    might guess—
but the climate being so chilly
their near nakedness swings
the balance of sympathy

for at least
      one shivering minute
over toward the eaters

hostilities

The Spanish explorer Heceta 1775
lost seven men to Indians
who wanted their boat
only so as to remove the nails

Capt. Hanna made the first trip
on skin business
1785 from China
inaugurated the skin trade
in a fight with the Nootkan people

1787 Barkley lost a boat crew of 5
1788 attack on Gray at Murderers Harbor
Same year attack on Meares in Strait of Fuca
Kendrick attacked at Barrell Sound 1791
same summer Gray lost his mate Joshua Caswell
and 2 men in the North

Indian plot to seize the *Clayoquot* 1792
seizure of the *Boston* at Nootka 1803
and massacre of all but Jewitt and Thompson
8 men of the *Atahualpa* lost 1805
crew of the *Tonquin* massacred 1811

Along the line many warriors also died
 (statistics missing or incomplete)

the character of the Ahts

'The prominent characteristics which I have ob-
served in the Ahts are a want of observation, a great
deficiency of foresight, extreme fickleness in their
passions and purposes, habitual suspicion, and a
love of power and display. Added to which may be
noticed their ingratitude and revengeful dispositions,
their readiness for war, and revolting indifference to
human suffering. A murder, if not perpetrated on one
of his own tribe, or on a particular friend, is no more
to an Indian than the killing of a dog, and he seems
altogether steeled against human misery, when
found among ordinary acquaintances or strangers.
The most terrible sufferings, the most pitiable
conditions, elicit not the slightest show of sympathy,
and do not interrupt the current of his occupations or
his jests for a moment.'

—Gilbert Malcolm Sproat,
Scenes and Studies of Savage Life, 1868

drifting

Well we should have known
it was all over with cant of empire
those snowy diamond mornings up
at the top of the world
above the Sound's unnavigable reaches
that sky looked so clean and true
just because the air's so
clear at that altitude
Rousseau couldn't have foreseen
these unimaginable latitudes
from the ship the peaks
brooding above impassable inlets
we sent the pinnace up
that came drifting back down empty

the drive

Always want to go deeper farther
out or in—to be real not virtual
part of one was afraid
but stronger than fear
was the desire to
            confront the Other
to trade with the interior
to encounter the Nimpkish
to follow those trails over
to Gold River
            and Woss Lake

                        (pierce darkness
                        to the heart)

3
THE RACE BEGINS

incoming

The 'port' of Nootka post-Cook almost
like those old Cold War movies
where you see the big board
at Strategic Air Command lit
up with incoming missiles

1785–1789 fourteen British
ships trading in
skins to the NW Coast
five launched from London the rest

Bombay Calcutta Canton Macao
not so much a strategy
of Empire as a pattern
of interest 'homing' on Nootka

the race begins

free enterprise pried open what
secrecy of Empire had controlled
Spanish held skin news close
no discovery diaries till Cook's
people disclosed their windfall
kicked off the race to the coast
the rush on soft gold

1785   Capt. Jas. Hanna in the *Harmon* aka *Sea Otter*

'The man who had
undertaken to conduct his
little band of Argonauts
in an almost untried course' (Meares)

attacked in plain light of day
by Indians at Nootka
a chisel was stolen
Hanna retaliated
'with considerable slaughter'

20 Indians dead

Hanna offered medical help to the wounded

resumed trade

came away with 560 skins

net $20,600 in China

Hanna's practical joke

Hanna invited Maquina
aboard the *Sea Otter*   the chief
was given a stately

seat a chair on deck to sit on
beneath which gun powder
had been sprinkled

royal prerogative
a doubtful privilege when
the pile of black sand

under him was contacted
by the burning fuse
that trailed across the deck

blast and flash
lifted the Sun King clear
of the deck and left

scars on his backside
he later showed the Spanish
to attest the offense

against his dignity
which he said had provoked
his attempt on the ship

the Scotsman

Hanna's second voyage, in a new *Sea Otter*
outfitted at Macao
120 ton snow with thirty
men and better guns but late
arriving Nootka August 1786
beaten to the punch by Strange

shunted off first N then S
'traded' (entailed)
his name away to an Indian chief
at Clayoquot
—Chief Cleaskinah
of Ahousat—
yet kept it

able to get only 50 skins at Nootka
50 more elsewhere on the coast
after all that trouble
vended at $50 / piece
with three hundred odd
fragments cheaper   profits
                     off 60%
          total $8000

'Before he could
engage in a third,
this active and able
seaman was called
to take that voyage from

whence there is no return'

of a fever alone nameless
in an Asian port

Portlock & Dixon

Second independent venture on the Coast
                         11 mos. after Hanna
Portlock & Dixon   1785–86

George Dixon with Cook's *Resolution*
                             and *Discovery*
armourer's mate—metal worker (Indians
                         want metal)
an able man
seeking command
    was charged with the *Queen Charlotte*

and Nathaniel Portlock
midshipman under Cook went on
    to China with Gore & King
took company boat upriver to Canton
to deliver skins
            was given the *King George*

the backer Richard Cadman   (Cadmus
                Etches   sowed the dragon's
                       teeth)

Dixon's Voyages

'The fur trade
is inexhaustible
wherever there
are inhabitants'
      —Dixon's *Voyages*

white men needed
    Indians
to do the killing

both principals
at this early date
considered the otter
    inexhaustible

Capt. Portlock, of London

'Having discovered the Indians on the border of Nootka Sound, who had so far advanced from their savage state as to refuse to sell to Mr. Strange, for any price, the peltry which they had already engaged to Mr. Hanna, these enterprises have ascertained this exhilarating truth to mankind, that civilization and morals must forever accompany each other!'

Portlock proclaimed

Portlock proclaimed the early voyages
a useful education to the Nootkans
in civilized commercial practice
salutary development for the trade
and inevitable as December rain
in that place (he wrote) the first enterprises
considering the small capital and great risks
brought profits not enviously great
yet enlarged the limits of discovery
made navigation more safe
on the North Pacific ocean and above
all this taught the American savages
that Strength must always subordinate to discipline

Capt. Dixon's killing   1786–1787

Portlock & Dixon's
2nd voyage   sea otter skins total sold
China at end of expedition   2552

the competition   ———————-   to date
    Hanna   down to end of 1787
    Strange   combined total
    Meares   of all voyages:
    Barkley   2841 skins

one trip Dixon netted
in China $54,857 paid

why the British gave the trade up

South Sea Co. East
India Co. understood
Empire as their cut

Portlock & Dixon
brought back
2500 skins

but Etches
took a loss
on what monopoly

scraped off the top—
why British
gave the trade up

Marchand loses his shirt
(French withdrawal from the coast)

La Perouse 1786 round the globe
a thousand skins $10,000 in China
proposes a great French skin factory
'fifty leagues along the sea-shore'
but warns of over-supply
Marchand meets Portlock 1788
goes out to the coast 1790
collects an abundance of skins
but is refused entry in China—
temporary market glut—
has to bring his skins
home to be eaten by worms in Lyons

Strange

James Charles Stewart Strange
traded an adze and a saw to Maquina
for a house to put
his sick people in

first British property acquisition NW Coast

got 'every rag of fur within
the Sound, and for a Degree
to the Northward and Southward of it'

godson of Bonnie Prince Charlie
out of Empire   black sheep
        entailed a contempt
        pour la sauvage—their
        (les sauvages)   'nobility'

eating vermin & drinking blood

the magic of black sand

Strange passed
off on the chief
the theory that
guns only worked
when white men fired them
but proof was required

filled up a musket
with too much powder
to prove his point
gave it to the chief
to shoot flash whiplash
knocked the Sun King
on his ass kept
the mystique going
a season longer

the magic of black sand
and its repercussions
backlash of guns
in the Indian's hand

Maquina's muskets would
one day number thousands

one blast

one blast of the strange musket may
once have knocked Maquina on his back
but when McKay tried that
a second time the chief
grabbed the musket   that was that
McKay's hands were shaking
'the want of courage
                    (stranded among
                    the Americans!)
soon lost him the respect
of the hardy and sagacious
savages   neither daring
nor ingenious he gradually fell
in their esteem and was
at last totally despised'

McKay

McKay—
the bewildered and distressed
ex Royal Navy
(black sheep) Irish
surgeon's mate
left by Strange
as 'agent'
among the Nootkans
to 'go native'
(extrication from
'the system
as given')
appropriately
rescued by
Barkley's
IMPERIAL EAGLE
(Austrian colors out of Ostend)

going wild

When Barkley sailed into Nootka
in the *Imperial Eagle*
he found John McKay filthy
starving half out of his head
after his hard times among the Nootkans
surviving on a few handfuls of garden peas
some dried fish heads
and a store of putrid whale blubber
had seen decapitated
human heads on spikes as trophies
'his observation so much circumscribed
he could give no account of this
curious people with whom he had lived
fourteen months in habits of closest intimacy'

for a long time

For a long time after the apparition
Resolution and *Discovery*
an elder moon shone
                        over the ocean
vanishing conception   Spanish luna
'Shunning to Indian
                        no good'
like being a slave in the Indian nation
extrication from the system as given
'escape' makes no sense to an Indian
if by escape you mean
willingly removing yourself from
                        the condition
John McKay thought he might
                        advance himself
by dropping out of civilization
the black sheep
                chased out into Empire
the ocean spoke to him in
                the wave wash
and said, 'Resignation'

4
S<small>PHERES</small> <small>OF</small> I<small>NTEREST</small>

an enterprising rogue

Strange beaten out at Cook's Inlet
by Tipping in the latest ship to be named
Sea Otter (Bengal Fur Society, Calcutta)
owner John Meares   erstwhile naval man
ex-lieut. R. N.   entrepreneur adventurer
enterprising rogue   charming liar
Indiaman sans principle
sailor sans funds   professional scoundrel
manipulated rhetoric of Empire
to his own dubious ends
fixers, hucksters, puffers, go-betweens
merchant investors
schemes & scams   Meares'
1786 syndicate bought
Sea Otter & Nootka   Bengali
opium to Malacca   Dutch entrepôt
scurvy & strong drink
flying false flag   Portugese colors
desperado of wild & pathless seas

Meares the duplicit

Meares the duplicit   instigator of Pitt's
propaganda gambit   the manufactured
'crisis'   counterposing British interests
against Spanish (the 'Spanish armament'
or phony war)   first to claim land
rocky shore   island   inlets   fjords
as English   'bought' Nootka from Maquina
for either a pair of pistols (Meares' account)
or 8 or 10 sheets of copper (Duffin's)   stole other
captains' charts   appropriated discoveries
built the *Northwest America* at Friendly Cove

grifter

Meares inflated his settlement
at Nootka in his account of it
to exaggerate his property claim

His fellow grifter Duffin
complicit in the scam
testified their spread consisted

of 'a house of appartments'
with bed chambers, sheds & workshops
whereas the Portugese captain *de ruse*

of the *Ifigenia Nubiana*
called it 'very small
made with a few Indian boards'

the liar

Maquina contradicted Meares
and said the only thing
                                    he gave
away for the copper was
                                    sea otter skins
Maquina's name for Meares was
Aita-Aita (Liar)

irony

Indians showed Meares
such a sleight of hand in getting
iron materials
as was hardly to be conceived
irony of their love of metal
when their great craft skill was in wood
'It has often been observed
when the head of a nail
either in the ship or boats
stood a little without the wood
they would apply their teeth
in order to pull it out'

Meares educated Wickaninish

Meares educated Wickaninish in trading
Wickaninish the great potentate of Clayoquot
from whom Capt. Meares procured
such an excellent bargain in skins   June
1788 in course of a 'diplomatic
visit' (haggling session) Meares pulled
out two copper tea kettles   Wickaninish
ordered him to place same as 'gifts'
in the royal coffers   'large wooden chests
rudely carved & fancifully adorned
with human teeth'   fifty men came
forward each with a sea otter skin 'near
six feet in length and of the most jetty
blackness'   the chief made a speech
and gave his hand in friendship ('the
return he proposed to make for our
present')   skins valued in China
c. 2500 gold dollars

instructions in trading for skins

Preferred currency—late '80s

Indians asked for
'toes'—iron
chisels with blades
on one end—drove
hard bargains—
they are great
chiselers said Richard
Cadman Etches
the backer
of Capt. Meares   in caveat—
such intelligent traders
that should you be in the least
degree inattentive
they will so enhance
the value
of their skins as
not only to exhaust
your present
stock but also
to injure
if not ruin
any future adventures

early phase of the trading

It may be the Indians didn't
   think quite as much of Meares' 'gifts'
   as Meares supposed from their friendliness

At Nootka they pinched
   a grindstone from his house
He had them kept out
They went off to another bay to fish
   but some snuck back to the cove
   at night and pinched the ship's pinnace
They broke the pinnace up to get the nails

More things turned up missing
   than Meares could count

Maquina still protested
   his fidelity to his friend

Collision Course: 1789
(don Estéban José Martínez)

His Imperial Catholic Majesty
crowded by the English
tending Spain's sphere of interest
headed off the interloper
a long way from Madrid and Mexico
distance even further if
young wife home in Andalusia
flowers in her hair
Martínez the Sevillano
1774 second pilot under Pérez
shadow over his career promise
questions of competence
conduct unbecoming an officer
implications of tippling
in public in private
violent dispute with his pilot
López de Haro
outside Prince William Sound
1778 Alaska
sailed erratic courses
consorted with Russians
reciprocal banquets all around
fresh meat black bread vodka
ham cheese chocolate brandy
accused of outrages
aboard the *Princesa*
his word against López de Haro's
yet appointed to command
the crucial Nootka mission

'sacrificing my last breath'
recommended occupation
'by carrying this out we gain
possession of the land
between the port of Nootka
and San Francisco
and dominion
over a multitude of Indians'
pursuance of discovery's
questionable rights
in his unsteady hand

Imperial Skin Dreams
(Viceroy Flores sends Martínez
back up north, 1789)

Spain must colonize outposts on the coast
keep the skin trade
out of foreign hands
Russians must be evicted
English and Americans
headed off at the pass

Advantages of skin
dealing evident now to Spain
time to mind the shop
send Mexicans up north
populate Alaska

'The number of vagrants of both sexes
in Mexico City alone
would give us useful families
for the greater part of this'

Charges against the hard drinking
Sevillano suspended
one last chance to
redeem his naval career

in the eyes of God and King

Diplomacy at Sea (May 5, 1789)

When the anchor was dropped
Spanish colors were run up
Franciscans led the men in prayer
Andalusians of the quarter deck
Mexican Indians before the mast
gratitude being owed to
Nuestra Señora del Rosario
echo of fifteen big guns saluting
three cheers to his Imperial
Majesty Carlos around the Sound
resounding   mistaken
by the Scottish trader
Meares' man Douglas on
the *Ifigenia Nubiana*
as a welcoming salvo in his honor

and this also shall be given us

Beneath the tawny port of a warm sundown
Clouds in the masts take on the structures
Exemplified by space of a woman's bones
Calm lies the Sound under Venus rising
Orange goings down of great suns prelude
The light in which a flying fish catches them
Nights of the ocean in which your shrouding's
Caught as if it were in its own reflection
His cruise having lasted all this long while
There are the summer night's Scarlatti
On the quarter deck under Pacific stars
And skins coming aboard in slim canoes
A coat of otter fit for a mandarin
In exchange for fishhooks and teapot lids

by the sound

Scarlatti on the quarterdeck   the Sevillano

    pungent oranges   bright green wings

Spanish brandy

       impatience   but the wave wash

  rushing of wind among red cedars

  and continuous soft sound of

Indian polishing   otter canoe

        glassy hull

   for silent running

  up beach   like foghorn

Some small bird calling from sleep

122

Naming Ceremony at Nootka
(May 1789)

Maquina's giving-a-name-to-his-son
ceremony
Martínez and the Franciscans
honored guests
Indians in red ochre paint
and crazy feathers danced
drumming on planks
echoed through the house
Chief Kelekum
and Chief Maquina
threw off their bear skins
put on sea otter robes
the boy too wore sea otter
celebration chants resounded
kept Martínez awake
back aboard the *Princesa*

retentiveness

Chief Kelekum of Nootka
married the sister of Chief
Wickaninish of Clayoquot

One of Martínez' men
killed Kelekum with
his wife looking on

Kelekum's wife went
to live with Wickaninish
a bad stink stuck to

The name Martínez
among the Indians of
the Coast after this

Maquina's exile

The Iberian Quimper
found Maquina taking refuge
with inlaws in Clayoquot
at the lodge of Wickaninish
with its ninety-foot roof timbers
supported by giant carved figures
forming a doorway mouth

no mention of troubles with Martínez
over his baby eating
or the murder of Kelekum
the exiled king rose
made a very natural bow
'*amigo, amigo*'

prisoners in the eastern ocean

Martínez slapping the English
sea dogs into irons—Meares' men
Douglas   Hudson   Colnett
'robbed me   in as gentle a manner
as he possibly could'
rival authority   distant imperial
kings   George   Carlos
behind immediate guns
little English coasting vessels
at the mercy
of Spanish naval ships
the brig *San Carlos* (López de Haro)
the corvette *Princesa* (Martínez)
seized the *Argonaut*
took Colnett's 84 sheets
of precious trading copper
and the makings of the sloop *Jason*
dispatched the crews
to misery in Mexico
mosquitos   fever   heat
to illustrate the perfidy of the English
the tragedy of Henry VIII
was played in the town plaza
at Tepic   Colnett
going bonkers
'even the young lady
that acted Ann Bullen
prefer'd acting the more
amorous part of Henry's Character
with some of my Officers in Private'

The Spanish Armament
(Nootka crisis 1789)

Martínez' seizure of Colnett's ship
provocation
                    or pretext?
'the Spanish Armament'

empires armed to the teeth
                    sea dragon's
                              big guns

Pitt banking on Meares'
                    dubious 'evidences'?

Lord Howe
Admiral of the Fleet
patrolling the Atlantic
with 9 frigates
and 29 ships of the line

64 ships of the line
and 43 frigates
of his Imperial
Catholic Majesty
maneuvering
off Cadiz
and Cartagena

31 Spanish ships of the line
and 9 frigates
at sea

everyone's mind
on distant
little Nootka

wrestling for Empire

When Great Britain and Spain
bumped heads over 'the cat skins of Nootka'
Martínez seized Colnett's ship
Pitt sent off ultimatums—at dawn

press gangs descended
upon (busted into) pubs
inns and doxy
houses of English ports

to drum up warship companies
to battle with the Spanish
a diplomatic note
to the ambassador

confirmed 'unquestionable right'
of British subjects on NW Coast
to 'a free and undisturbed enjoyment
of the benefits of commerce'

Superior Orders (October 1789)

'Haro: I have departed Nuca by
superior order to San Blas'
—Estéban José Martínez

The long love that in my thought doth harbor
How far from port with how much longer to go
For that matter how far from sherry or madeira
All that is lost and fallen ought to be
Who'd explain loyalty to fate and brandy
Indians among our crew dispirited by the cold
So much harsher than autumn in Mexico
Days of obscurity and foul prevailing weather
Rain fog and the progress of worm in planks
Closing off whatever had appeared our goal
We'll abandon everything we've built or meant to
Though the rice begins to produce the wheat is planted
All through the long New World shadowed afternoon
We warp out of the cove preparatory to sailing

opportunists

Carlos flinched first
then East India
Co. had English
traders' hands tied

Boston men snuck in
by the back door   coasting
in small ships
        sloops
        brigs
& snows

5
<u>A</u>MONG THE <u>A</u>MERICANS

The Architect
(first voyage of the **Columbia**, *1789)*

Charles Bulfinch architect
built Boston up
the first Yankee
trip to the Coast was
planned at his
father's house
with stake money
also from Joseph
Barrell a neighbor
a trader struck
by what Cook had related
'There is a rich
harvest to be reaped
by those
who shall first go in'

in this year

'In this year the Venetians refused to make
war on the Milanese because they held
that any war between buyer and seller
must prove profitable to neither'
                                   —Burckhardt

On this principle Boston men
some from the best families
(an honorable and mobile trade)
sought peace with
the aboriginal people

What every able-bodied seaman must know:
the old-time art of rigging
splicing seizing parceling grafting
pointing worming serving
and how to haggle with the Indians

Cargo in Trading Goods
(1st Voyage of Columbia)

Hoes	36	
Shingling Hatchets	91	
Large Axes	73	
Small Axes	34	
Adzes	49	
Pole Axes	26	
Bill Hooks	52	
Hatchetts	115	
Drawing Knives	78	
Rat Traps	18	
Snuff Bottles	78	
Butchers Knives	117	
Cod Hooks	52	Gross
Jews Harps	22	3/4 Dozn.
Tin Soldiers	6	Boxes
Trinketts	5	Boxes
Beads	116	lb.
Necklaces	15	Dozn.
Brass Pans	31	
Brass Tops	26	
Razors	18	Dozn.
Tobacco Boxes	72	
Tin quart potts	72	
Tin pint potts	191	
Tin half pint potts	125	
Dippers	23	
Tile potts	38	
Egg Slicers	19	
Tin Kettles	12	

Pepper Boxes	16	
Pudding pans	2	
Polish'd Iron pint potts	8	
Sail Needles	600	
Looking Glasses	461	
Pint Basons	12	
Combs	50	Dozn.
Awl Blades	6	Gross
Awl Hafts	6	Dozn.
Cuttoes	1476	
Shering Knives	55	
Reaping Hooks	3	
Pump Hamers	8	
Hand Saws	72	
Pewter Porringers	72	
Basons	72	[Quart]
Elegant earings	14	Dozn. pr.
Large Saws	7	
Lott Wire	1	[Bale]
Cloathing	12	Suits
Brass Tobacco Boxes	9	
Tinder Boxes	34	
Skillitts	90	
Spiders	95	
Iron Potts and Kettles	84	
Kane Knives	37	
Chizells	1600	

Like a Living Flame
(August 9, 1790)

First Americans round the Horn
went for skins found a strange world
Gray's *Columbia* back from
the Coast and China via Owyhee
came in Boston Harbor firing
the federal salute thirteen guns
returned by three huzzas a hearty
round of applause from a great
concourse of the citizens of Boston
assembled on the several wharves
marching along grandly behind Captain
Gray in the parade of welcome
through city streets to Governor John
Hancock's mansion Ottoo
the Sandwich Islander in
a long cloak of golden suns
set in blazing scarlet crested
with a feather helmet moved up
State Street like a living flame

Boston men take over

'so many of the vessels engaged in this (skin) trade belonged here, the Indians had the impression that Boston was our whole country'
                                        —Capt. Sturgis of Boston

1790–1818   22 English   on NW
                   108 American vessels   coast

Perkins Lamb Dorr Boardman Lyman Sturgis
many a Boston family owes its
fortune to the empire of skin
not a few captains who
came in through the hawse-hole
each officer enjoys 'primage'
one to eight percent net proceeds of trip
plus 'the privilege' homeward passage cargo space
for his personal take in silk and nankeens
encouraging the trade private adventuring
by age 19 John Boit captain of his own ship
the sloop *Union* 89 tons to the Coast
for skins

REMARKS
on the Ship Columbia's voyage from Boston,
(on a voyage, round the Globe)
by JOHN BOIT,   fifth officer

I am born with a love of the sea in my *Blood*, being a son of Massachusetts; this even the Boston *Latin* school cou'd not breed out of me.

October 8, 1790

Crew appears to be a set of fine fellows. A brave Spirit maintains, though not till four years hence, and only with *Good Luck* at that, shall we have our next sight of home (or the Land of this side of the Continent). Some mourns (or misses) their wives, sweet Hearts or Mistrises; the younger men are left (with less difficulty) to revere their Mothers; while the Captain appears to resign himself to the consolations of his present female company Nancy the Goat (who has been round the World with him once already); as do those other among us who enjoy her Milk in the Cabbin!

November 25, 1790

Ship's crew are all in good health. Now 54 1/2 days from Boston, 25 days from Isle of Sal, (both these are thought quite *long* passages), their keeping in fair spirits is much to be consider'd. Keep all hands through the day (in good weather) employ'd in the various departments of the ship; it is best to keep them moving. They are allow'd tea or coffee each morning, and in generall the ships fare is good; but regret to say proper attention to airing their beds and cloathing and fumigating their berths is not paid, with the necesscary result vermin is plenty among them and not a few of the men now may be identifed (without *looking*) by their distinctive *smell.*

April 23, 1791

S. Latt—4° 37′ N. Long. 114° 39′. ☉ *Glory* to *God* in his sevrall and many Creatures. Between the hours of 3 and 4 PM departed this life our dear freind *Nancy* the *Goat.* Having been the Captain's companion on a former voyage round the Globe, Her spirited disposition for adventure led her to undertake a 2d voyage of Circumnavigation; But the various changes of Climate, and sudden transition from the Polar Colds to the tropical heats of the Torrid Zone, prov'd too much for a constitution naturally delicate, At 5 PM Committed her body to the deep. She was lamented by those who got a share of her *Milk*!! Men of War Birds and Porpoises round the Ship. Vast many marine birds flying round, the wide Tropic Sea and its abundant Life encompassing us, all appeared to share in our lament for *Nancy.*

June 4, 1791

N. Latt. 49° 10′ W. Long. 120° 21′. ☉ This day made the land, on the NW Coast of the American Continent between Nootka (or King Georges sound) and Clayoquot (or Coxes harbour). For these sevrall days past we had seen whales, Drift Wood, feathers, kelp, etc. All signs of its vicinity. Breakers Point bore NE by E 8 leagues, high land back, and snow perceivable on some of the higher mountains. A nobler Vista of this new World wou'd be difficult to conceive.

June 5, 1791

N. Latt. 49° 5´ *Correct* W. Long. 125° 26´. This day anchor'd in Coxes harbour and found itt very commodious. We tarry'd till the 16th June. This Harbour is made remarkable by three remarkable round Hills, abrest its entrance. An Indian call'd Captain Hannah, Cheif of the village *Ahouset,* who claim'd his name was the gift of a certain sea Captain, came on board and appear'd freindly. Above 300 Natives was along side in the course of the day. Their canoes was made from the hollow'd out body of a tree, with stem and stern pieces, neatly fixed on; these models seem'd of a remarkable seaworthiness not unlike our Nantucket whale boats and was *handled* by the Natives in a dexterous method that show'd them quite accomplish'd Seamen. The dress of these Indians was either the Skin of some animal, or else a Blankett of their own manufactory, made of some kind of Hair; This garment was slung over the right shoulder. They all appear'd very freindly, and brought us plenty of fish and Greens, which was greatly requir'd.

We landed the sick immediately on our arrivall and pitch'd a tent for their reception. There were ten of them in the last stage of the Scurvy, still they soon improv'd, upon smelling the turf, and eating Greens of various kinds; We buried sevrall of the sick men up to the Hips in the earth, and let them remain for *hours* in that situation. Found this method of great service in speeding their recovery.

140

The principall village in this harbour is call'd *Opitsat*, and is govern'd by *Wickaninish*, a warlike Cheif. He and his family visited us often. Itt appear'd *Wickanininsh*'s pow'r along this coast entitles him to a kind of *Tyranny* of the trade hereabouts, other Cheifs visiting us only through his Permission, or his family's; resolv'd therefore to make an Ally of him if at all possible.

The Indians brought sevrall *Deer*, and plenty of Rock Cod, Salmon, and other fish, Wild parsley, and a root call'd *Isau* or Isop by the natives and much resembling a small onion or leek, was brought us in abundance. We purchas'd many of the Sea Otter skins which are the principall object of our Voyage, in exchange for Copper and blue Cloth.

These Indians are of a large size, and somewhat Corpulent. The Men wear no other covering, but the garment before mentioned, and seem to have no sense of shame, as they appear in a state of Nature. The Women stand in great fear of the Males, but appear to be naturally very modest, their garment is manufactor'd from the bark of a Tree, a species of *caedar*, and is well executed, being so constructed as to cover them complete from the Neck to the *Ancle*. Both Male and Female wear *Hats* of a conicle form made out of strong reeds. On them is painted (in a rude but not unpleasing manner) their mode of Whale fishery.

Attoo, the Captain's servant (and a native of the Sandwich Isle) seem'd to place to great hopes in the Indians hospitality; He turning up Absent we was sure he had run away among them. A cheif called Tatoochkasettle then coming on board, we placed a guard over him, and sent his Canoe back to the village with the News. They soon returned with *Mr. Attoo,* and ransom'd their Cheif, who appear'd no little releiv'd at this rescue.

what Gray didn't know

what Gray didn't know
when he took Wickaninish's
brother Tootiscoosettle
ship's prisoner:
events of one year
earlier   the English
trader Colnett seized
then quickly seeing
his error released
that same chief   afterwards
Colnett's intention to
winter with the *Argonaut*
at Clayoquot became
problematic a New
Year's Eve Indian
attack made him
risk warping
out of the Sound in
horror seas at dawn

dependence on goods solely obtainable
from white man

'no skins could be purchased without ammunition & Fire
Arms. Their former weapons, Bows and Arrows, Spears
and Clubs are now thrown aside & forgotten...everyone
had his musket. Thus are they supplied with weapons
which they no sooner possess than they turn against the
donors.'
                          —Bell, of Vancouver's party

Wickaninish hog of display copper
had the outer harbors raked
for sea otter to buy hammered copper sheets
Wickaninish the hog of power
had the otter hunted into depletion
to furnish himself with
    200 muskets
        two barrels of powder
            and a considerable portion of shot
from that willing and open-handed Boston
man Captain Kendrick
compliant vendor
certain unhappy sailors (later)
were ultimate payees
of the violent fee

Report on Dangerous Customers
(Capt. Kendrick to Capt. Gray)

Treet the Natives with Respect where Ever you go
Cultivate frindship with them as much as possibel
and take Nothing from them But what you pay them
for according to a fair agreement,
and not suffer your peopel to affront them
or treet them Ill

Kendrick's son died at the hand of natives of Owyhee
Gray lost his second mate (Caswell)
to the Haidas at Murderers Harbor (Massacre Cove)

To barter so long as you could do business
among one or the other of the myriad
bays and coves and inlets
and then move on   Be sensible
and fair to the Indian
Never attempt to penetrate
into those fjords and inlets
beyond range of the ship's guns

A Most Savage Abomination (Boit)

August 10, 1791

N. Latt 55° 0′   W. Long. 133° 0′.   Port
Tempest bearing NE by N twelve leagues. Natives
brought us plenty of fine Otter furs. They go well
arm'd with bows, arrows and spears and appear to
be a *savage* race. Went in the Cutter, well arm'd,
to a small cove, not far distant from the Ship and
soon Caught 9 large Halibutt. The Ship was
conceal'd by a point of land making out from the
NE part of the Cove, this occasion'd some
uneasiness among our small party in the Cutter,
as we was breifly left expos'd; but saw no Canoes,
and went unmolested.

August 12, 1791

Still laying at anchor in same situation. The ship's
2d officer Mr. Caswell, this morning, took a
Boatswains Mate and one Seamen with him in the
Jolly Boat, by the permission of Capt. Gray, and
went to the *Cove* afishing. A breeze springing up
soon after, offering us the opportunity to leave this
place, a six pounder was fir'd, a Signal for the
boat to return. She not appearing, soon two more
Cannon was fir'd. Got the Ship under way and
stood off and on, and sent the pinnace under
charge of the 4th Officer Mr. Waters in search of
the small boat. Soon after, we saw the Pinnace
returning with the Jolly Boat in tow, without any
person in her and soon discover'd they had the
Boats Colours hoisted half mast; with this

melancholy token they approach'd the Ship. We soon discover'd our worthy freind and brother officer, (Mr. *Joshua Caswell* 2d) lay dead in the bottom of the boat, strip'd perfectly naked and stab'd in upwards of twenty places. Mr. Waters party inform'd us that upon rounding the point of the *Cove* they saw nothing of John Folger (the Boatswains mate) but saw Joseph Barnes (the Sailor) lay dead on the beach, likewise disfigur'd and quite naked. Fearing the Natives lay in *ambush*, they did not land to take off the Corps, thus leaving the poor dead Sailor, and it is highly probable also the Boatswains mate, to prospects of further indignity, a most *savage* Abomination such as remains generally reserv'd during the Warrs of *civiliz'd* Nations.

In Mr. Caswell I lost a firm and steady freind, he was a man of mild and gentle temper, a Complete Seaman, and in short was possest of every qualification that bespoke the Gentleman. Itt was observ'd that the day previous to this disastrous affair, few Indians had visited the Ship. Twas Resolv'd to double this Evenings watches in *precaution.*

August 3, 1791

N. Latt. 53° 43′   W. Long. 132° 23′.   Calm, and temperate weather. We lay off at the western entrance to the sound, on which Port Tempest is situated. Gave this unfortunate spot the name Murderers Cape. At 8 in the morning the 4th Officer Mr. Waters was dispatch'd with a party well arm'd in the Pinnace, for to dig a grave for our worthy freind Mr. Caswell. At 9 the pinnace return'd. At 10 Left the Ship with three boats, under charge of Mr. Hazwell, 1st Officer, Carrying the Corps, with the Ship firing minute guns. (To this doleful accompaniment), At 11 Capt. Gray landed in a small boat, and after performing divine service, we *inter'd* the remains of our departed, and much beloved, *freind*, with all the solemnity we was capable of. The place where this unhappy ceremony was accomplish'd was a gloomy spot at the mouth of a *rivulet* coming out of the Woods, and nothing was to be heard but the bustling of an aged oak whose lofty branches hung wavering o'er the grave, together with the meandering brook, the Cries of the Eagle wandering down above the drooping trees, and the weeping of his freinds added solemnity to the Scene.

Two White World Parties
(winter 1791–92)

Two white world parties on the Coast
Eliza, Alberni and the Nootka garrison
'The rain is the worst' noted the Spanish pilot
three-day downpours cold bones
holed up at Friendly Cove

Gray and the men of the *Columbia*
anchored in Clayoquot
struck camp for the winter
at Disappointment Inlet
opposite the ancient village Opitsat

At Anchor in Clayoquot Harbour:
Winter Quarters (Boit)

September 20, 1791

Lat. 49° 9′ N., Long. 125° 30′ W.   This Cove
was form'd by an Isle and the SE shore of
Clayoquot sound. Itt is so small that when the
Ship is Moor'd you might throw a stone the length
of the beach in any direction. The passages in was
found not to exceed 100 feet, so that we was in a
complete *bason*, safely enough shou'd any of that
Spanish *Sett* attempt to follow us in.

Sept. 20–Oct. 7, 1791

The Object of our proceedings during this period,
the *Adventure* was set up at the back of a fine
beach the woods being previously clear'd by our
Men. A Log House was erected near, mounted
with two Cannon, and *Loop* holes for Musketry.
The Captain as usual much given to damn
nonsense wou'd have it nam'd fort *Defiance*, tho it
was *generally* without much spirit to engage in
hostilities that we putt it up.

October 13, 1791

The frame of the Sloop is up Complete, and this
day brought the Garboard streak of Plank to her
bottom. *This* is what I call dispatch. *Wickaninish*,
high Cheif, came on board, with sevrall of the
royall family. To what did we owe this Honor? He
inform'd that his winter village *Okermina* was a
great way off, which occasion'd his visiting us

150

seldom. He went on Shore, and astonishment was conspicuous in his royall countenance at the work going on there. The Natives was very much puzzled to know how we shou'd get the Sloop off when finished, as she now sits 75 foot back from high water mark. Seeing the great interest they showed in this question we determined to exhibit a proportionate reserve in making our plans and Intentions apparent. The Captain yet appear'd to think it a *fine* thing to have so distinguished a Visitor, and bow'd and scrap'd to a point of damn nonsense. Some call this sound trading policy others among the Crew was privately *inclined* to call it Something else.

October 15, 1791

This my 16th birthday, second in the large World beyond the fires of *Home* and the small old Halls of Boston Latin school, I quietly celebrate while on watch among my *Thoughts* beneath the numerous starrs of the sound.

October 27, 1791

The Natives brought us some excellent Salmon. Experience much rain, which hinders the work. When the weather is too bad for to work on the Sloop, keep the Carpenters under shelter making a *boat* for her. Heard of three *Spanish Ships* being at Nootka. Keep always upon our guard against supprize as we are among a powerful Sett. Took the boat out after Game. Met with some *Indians* that was a little troubelsome, they endeavour'd to take the *Captain's* coat from the boat, but with the firing of a musket over their heads they was soon convinced to go off. When detach'd parties of our men are encounter'd in a vulnerable Situation, a reasonable *Prudence* must prevail over our *generally* freindly motives toward these Natives, who might otherwise deceive themselves into thinking any *Opportunity* cou'd be turned to their Advantage.

Wickaninish complained

Wickaninish complained
to Capt. Josiah Roberts of
the *Jefferson*
Gray had threatened
to fire on his people

Wickaninish said
Gray lent him a coat
then demanded repayment in skins

Is this the same coat the Indians had seized
from Gray's boat
and returned only when
Boit pointed the gun at them?

Excursions to Opitsat   *(Boit)*

December 22, 1791

Capt. Gray went on his own advisement to Opitsat an Indian Village for to look at a Cheif, said to be very sick. On his arrivall he was rec'd very *cordially* and conducted to the sick mans house, which was full of people. In one Corner lay the Sick Cheif, and arround him eight strong men, which kept pressing his stomach with their hands, and making a most hideous *Bow-wowing*, in the poor fellows ears. Upon the Captains approach, he suppos'd the Cheif to be nearly dead, and order'd this band of Doctors to desist, having made him some *gruell* to take. The Cheif soon came too a little, and order'd two Sea Otter skins given to the Captain as a present. After giving a Wine toast the Captain order'd him to be left to sleep, and went off to visit a number of Cheifs houses, the masters of which treated him with an attention not very common among savages. (he *return'd on board.*)

I made an excursion to this same Village not long after. As soon as I landed, Men, Women, and Children came down to the beach to receive me. They made no offer to molest the boat. Found the Cheif much better, and releived from his pressing and noisy freinds. (learn'd his name to be *Yethlan,* youngest brother of *Wickaninish.*) The house was large and commodious, and wou'd hold fifty *Indians* very comfortably, sevrall families appear'd to occupy itt at once, all round was packages of Fish in *Boxes*, fashion'd of wood, and decorated with *pearl shells*; Their furniture consisted cheifly of *matts*, and wooden boxes, which last serves also to boil their fish in, which they easily do by applying red hot stones, till it boils. They neither scale or draw the fish, but as it comes from the water so it goes into the box, to boil, or on the Coals to broil; there was sevrall fires about the house but there being no chimnies, the smoke was *too mighty* for my eyes. They sleep on boards, rais'd about a foot from the ground, and Covered with Matts, rolling themselves up with furs. Over the sick man's head, there was a board cut out in the shape of a heart, and stuck full of Otter's teeth. A long spear was laid at each side of him. His young wife did not appear to be afflicted at the sight of her sick husband, but the Father and Mother was watching their Son with the most parentall affection. This certainly cou'd not have been feign'd for my visit, and was indeed affecting to observe. After boiling the sick man some rice and leaving more with his mother, I left the village and return'd safe on board.

December 25, 1791

This day was kept in mirth and festivity by all the *Columbia's Crew*, and the principall Cheifs of the sound by our invitation din'd on board ship. The Natives took a walk around the work shops on shore; They was suppriz'd at seeing three tier of wild fowl roasting at one of the houses—indeed we was a little suppriz'd at the novelty of the sight ourselves, for there was at least 20 Geese roasting at one immense fire. A fresh hogshead of old New England Rum and a Baril of Cyder was tapped.

The Ships Crew appear'd very happy, most of them being happy simply to be on shore. The Indians cou'd not understand why the Ship and houses was decorated with spruce bows. At 12 Clock fir'd a fedrall Salute, and ended the day toasting our *sweethearts* and *wifes*; and *may we* live to kiss them again the Ship's Sailmaker solemnly propos'd, To which though in much seeming consternation over his meaning our Native guests concurred politely.

January 1, 1792

This day being down sound, with the jolly boat after game, I again stop'd at the village of *Opitsat*. Visited *Yethlan* the sick Cheif, and found him much better. The family treated me extremely well. A similar hospitableness in a *Civiliz'd* nation wou'd be a matter for remark. I receiv'd many pressing invitations form the rest of the Cheifs for visiting their houses, and complied with most of them. Was particularly pleased at visiting *Wickaninish's* dwelling, who this day was giving a grand Entertainment to all the warriors of his Villages, with many visiters on hand from distant Villages. As soon as the *King* saw me I was call'd towards him and seated upon his right, the Privilege of a guest of honor. This house fashion'd of great Logs and planks was about 80 foot Long, and 40 broad, and about 12 feet high, with a flat roof. The *King* sat upon a platform elevated about two feet higher than the company, with a Canopy over his head, stuck full of animals teeth. The teeth of Sea Otters and other animals serving with these Indians a decorative purpose to be perceived in this ceremonial Panoply, may *generally* possess also a Religious significance, which they have neglected (or determin'd not) to explain to us. The Company consisted of about 100 men, all considerably advanced in years. Itt appear'd these *elders* comprised the sevrall Cheifs and petty royallty of the Villages freindly to Wickaninish. The Women belonging to the House proper was contain'd meanwhile in an apartment by themselves, busily employ'd making their Bark Garment, the Machines for that purpose is not unlike the Looms with us. The Women are very neat and dexterous in this business as I observed, they persisted in their labors not heeding the sevrall activities going on round them. The main dining course of the entertainment, which consisted of Fish Spawn mixed with Berries and train Oil, was served up in wooden Bowls handed by the lower Orders of males. I was invited strongly to partake, but the Smell was enough, therefore pleaded indisposition for to not give offence. After the elders had din'd, the remains was sent to the *females*, they seem not overmuch given to *Chivalry* in this respect. The King inform'd me they was going to have a dance in the evening, and wish'd for me to stay. I felt I had little to fear from them, but was expected back on board; was press'd, However declin'd and return'd on board.

January 17, 1792

Began to caulk the Sloop *Adventure*'s bottom, itt being now completely planked up. This day made another excursion to the Village, having this time put ourselves under the care of *Tatoochkasettle*, one of the King's brothers, who conducted us in his Canoe. Upon arrival was treated as usual very politely. Took up residence at *Tatoochkasettles* house, who invited a large Company. After supper finding I wish'd to visit some other familys this cheif sent his servants with lighted Torches for to conduct me. I return'd back about Midnight and found there was an excellent watch kept throughout the village, each watchman hooping at certain intervalls throughout the night. Whether this was a customary Practice of the natives or one occasion'd by my presence I was left to *wonder*. My Indian Freind had made me as comfortable a berth to sleep on as was in his power, but the House being full of smoak, and the Young Children very fractious, occasion'd my sleeping but little all night. I lay awake sensible of the squalling of the Infants and the Hooping of the *watch*, remarking on these curious events.

Mutual Incomprehension
(Columbia *at Clayoquot, 1791–92)*

Violation of the mourning
ceremonial when Hoskins
insisted on visiting
the women in lamentation

Degradation of the potlatch
when Gray failed
to accept the invitation
to Wickaninish's feast

When the Indian
plot hatched who could
unravel the causation
in the dark

long memories

Wickaninish no forgiver after all
offenses ought not to go unpunished
the threat of action against the insulter
is intended to deter future offense   injury unavenged
will be compounded by future aggressions
and Wickaninish was an implacable rememberer
Gray once his Hawaiian cabin boy
Ottoo ran off to the village and he took
hostage a noble kinsman of Wickaninish
should have known he would reap
trouble from the great chief

Wickaninish waited till midwinter had negotiated
time's pass outside village privation time
no longer seemed to move   believing them
in his trust the chief massed three thousand brave
attackers   the offensive undermined
by the confession of the confused Ottoo
on whose collusion Wickaninish had counted
giving the Boston men reason to be vigilant on
the night of the war hoops   and save their lives
to sail south and find the Columbia's mouth

The Plot Foiled   (Boit)

January 17, 1792

> We understand from the *Natives* that they some-
> times make Human sacrafices, and shocking to
> relate, that they eat the flesh of such poor *victims.*
> However I beleive that this Custom is not very
> common and only happens on some very particu-
> lar Occasion. A prisoner of War is the person
> selected for this savage feast.

February 18, 1792

> This day sevrall cheifs came on board, one of
> which we found was busily employ'd talking with
> our Sandwich *Island* lad. Their conversation was
> soon put a stop too, and the *Lad* examined, but he
> deny'd that the Cheif ask'd him any improper
> questions. These Natives, for the most part
> behaving so freindly, have occasion'd us to place
> too much confidence in them, and what a pity it
> is, that we cou'd not leave this port with that
> opinion of them which we had heretofore held; But
> alas! We now find them out to be still a savage
> tribe, through this Season of our residence in this
> place having only been waiting an opportunity to
> Massacre the *whole* of us in cold blood.

> This Opportunity we now have our own mistaken
> *Trust* to blame for having afforded them. The Ship
> had been brought some days previous to this to a
> bluff point of the Rocks, where she lay'd as to a
> *wharf,* not even touching the ground at low water.

The Cannon and all the stores was landed here, as we was about hauling on the Beach to grave and pay the Bottom. The Capt. gave this Order on Feb. 3 saying to the Officers of the Ship our *unloading* woul'd thus be made easier. The Ships clerke Mr. Hoskins perhaps mindful of his loyallty to our Owners objected to the captains plan saying the hauling of the Ship on the beach wou'd leave her out of sight of the *Block* house, but the Capt. remain'd unsway'd, insensible of the protests whisper'd among some of the Crew.

The situation of the *Ship* at this period was very favorable to the Natives views, and must have encouraged them with the hope of destroying the whole of us, without the loss of a man on their side. However in this they wou'd have been mistaken as, for all the late seeming freindly transactions between the *Natives* and us, we yet kept a strong watch, under the conduct of an Officer, and was always guarded against supprize. Still any suspected suspension of our vigilance wou'd have caused provocation, having greatly underestimated their *Numbers*. And shou'd we have been *over powr'd* by numbers, our freinds at home perhaps never wou'd have *known* our Sad fate.

It was therefore fortunate, that in the evening of the cheifs visit to the ship, the Sandwich Island lad made a Confession to his Master (as follows). He reported that *Tatoochkasettle*, (*the Cheif*) told him, that Wickaninish was about to take the Ship and Massacree all the Crew, and said he shou'd be a great man, if he wou'd wet our *Musketts*, and steal for him some *Bulletts*; He said they shou'd come that night or the next, and told him to come over to them when the fray first began. This news alarm'd the Ships Company exceedingly, and we immediately got in readiness to receive them. Capt. Gray call'd his Officers together for to consult what was best to be done, and we was unanimously of opinion, that 'twas best to haul the Ship on the ways, and Grave her, as the tide then suited; so doing we cou'd retreat in safety to the Block House, (where we had sevrall *Cannon* mounted and good *quarters*,) shou'd the Natives appear. This plan was immediately put in execution, leaving a strong guard on the point for to guard the *Stores* with nessescary signals shou'd they want releif. By midnight the Graving of one side of the Ship was finish'd, when we heard a most hideous hooping of *Indians*. At ev'ry shout they seem'd to come nearer, every man immediately took his arms, and stood ready both on board ship and at the Log house. They kept hooping about one hour, these noises greeted as cheerfully as we cou'd; after that time they ceas'd and 'tis probable retreated, lamenting their hard luck that the Cruell plan was so completely frustrated. Our guard at the *point* had seen many large Canoes off the entrance of the Cove, but like brave fellows, they had scorn'd to quit their Station; and it is to this we suppose we owe our Providential sparing from *attack*.

After this no more of the Natives visited Adventure Cove except some old women and young girls, who brought us berries and fish, and most probable they was sent as *Spies*.

February 22, 1792

> Launch'd the sloop *Adventure*. She went off admirably. Took a hawser and got her along side the ship, and soon had her rig'd.

March 4, 1792

> This day the Ship *Columbia* was completely rig'd, Hold stowed, and in every respect in readiness for sea. She look'd like a *fiddle!* The Kings Mother came along side and brought some Otter Skins which we purchas'd. She told Captain Gray that the *Moon* inform'd her son if he came to the Ship, he wou'd be kill'd.

avenging angel

March 27, 1792

> I am sorry to be under the nessescity of remarking
> that this day I was *sent* with three boats, all well
> man'd and arm'd, to destroy the village of Opitsat.
> It was a Command I was in no ways tenacious to
> execute.

When Gray launched the sloop *Adventure*
Americans walked away from Haswell's fort
could hardly have cherished much thought
of further use of the place Gray having
sent Boit with three boats to exact
the cost of Wickaninish's assault
the largest Indian village on the Coast
'Upwards of two hundred houses
generally well built for Indians
Every door that you entered in resemblance
to a human or beasts head
the passage being through the mouth
        (a circus of representation)
besides which much more crude carved work
some of it by no means inelegant
This fine Village the Work of Ages
was in a short time totally destroyed
the inhabitants having only lately & hastily fled'

Having Destroyed Opitsat
the Work of Time and Ages

Gray emptied his guns into the war canoe
so effectually as to kill—as Boit said—
or wound every soul in it
She drifted alongside the ship
Boit and the others pushed her clear
She drove to the north side of the Cove
under the shade of the trees
the April moonlight shone
upon the shade of the trees so brightly
a deep green against the silver
of the waters of the Cove
and the woods echoed with
groans of dying Indians
whose bodies were stranded on shore
Boit saw canoes passing and repassing
alongside the ship all night
retrieving bodies

The Discovery of the Great River
(12 May, 1792: John Boit, aetat. 17)

'We saw an appearance of a spacious harbor abreast of the Ship, haul'd our wind for it, observ'd two sand bars making off, with a passage between them to a fine river. Out pinnace and sent her in ahead and followed the ship under short sail, carried in from 1/2 three to 7 fm. and when over the bar had 10 fm. water, quite fresh. The River extended to the NE as far as eye cou'd reach, and water fit to drink as far down as the *Bars*, at the entrance. We directed our course up this noble *River* in search of a Village. The beach was lin'd with Natives, who ran along shore following the Ship. Soon after, above 20 Canoes came off, and brought a good lot of Furs, and Salmon, which last they sold two for a board Nail. The furs we likewise bought cheap, for Copper and Cloth. They appear'd to view the Ship with the greatest astonishment and no doubt we was the first civilized people that they ever saw. At length we arriv'd opposite to a large village, situate on the North side of the River, about 5 leagues from the entrance. Capt. Gray named this river *Columbia*'s and the North entrance Cape Hancock, and the South Point, *Adams*. This River in my opinion wou'd be a fine place to set up a *Factory* for skins.'

6
THREE EMPIRES

The Interloper
(Tlupananootl's challenge, 1792)

i. the challenge

Tlupananootl old chief of a village up Sound
stepped in took absent Maquina's place
doing the honors of greeting
Malaspina at Nootka
threw a party for the Spanish ship
set up camp next to Malaspina's tent
sang clan epics 'all in a meter
Anacreontic' plus little plays 'a farce'
masques of his several wars   the combat
and his enemies' dismay
a performance fit to serve as a resumé
showing him a fellow to be reckoned with
singing and dancing
until the sun went down snoozing
Malaspina wondered: who let *him* in?

ii. looking for the chief

Where was Maquina?
                staying out of Yuquot
holed up back at a fishing inlet
after his trouble with Martínez
The Spanish long boats found him dug in
muskets fired on the beach braves lined up

shot off more gratuitous powder
the Spaniards showed patience
soon the king was down Sound drinking
tea on the imperial corvettes

iii. royal power reasserted

Down the beach Tlupananootl loitered
glowered overshadowed loser cranky
demanding excessive prices for skins
he put on a water spectacular
for Bodega the biggest canoe
anybody had ever seen
three circuits of all the ships
stood up and sang at length
came for dinner   'expressions
few, mien stupid'   whereas
Maquina's conversation was
'sagacious, clear'   'He always
occupies the first place
when he eats at my table'
the Limeño
Bodega recognized
the rival suzerainty
of Maquina of Nootka
ceremonially ratified
the Spanish deed
the chief in his conical
royal whaling topper
drained a glass of sherry
polished off the fish
soup with a spoon
attacked the *tays*
frixoles ('noble's beans')
with fork and knife like
'the best mannered

European you ever knew'
Bodega closed the deal with
a Spanish steel helmet
and coat of mail
which Maquina wore for trading

Two Destinies (the surveyors, 1792)

If it hadn't been for him Spanish
Oregon would go all the way up
to Alaska—and probably no hockey
Discovery and *Chatham*

George Vancouver, R. N.
a gentleman of King's Lynn
out one morning looking
for the Northwest Passage bumped in
to the *Sutil* and the *Mexicana*
two goletas from San Blas
out surveying   mapping
    the northern and the
        eastern limits
            of the New World

Meeting of Three Empires
(September 1792)

i. Vancouver and Bodega

George Vancouver   explorer and navigator
ventured up Tahsis Inlet with
Juan Francisco de la Bodega y Quadra
to visit Maquina's fishing village
three English pinnaces a Spanish launch
Vancouver the topographer of landscape
'winding inland by a deep valley'
                    between steep fjords
forests taller than masts
with fifes and drums   ship's musicians
        —'a martial solemnity'
'to the no small entertainment of the natives'—
to imitate the Indian custom played
'vociferous songs & plaintive airs'
        in the late summer twilight
Maquina came to dinner   a tent pitched
'in a fine meadow
        delightfully skirting
        a small bay'

ii. ceremony at Maquina's village

by light of day
boats paraded
colors of distant kings
then royal parley
in the chief's great lodge
on cedar mats

and bentwood
imperial regalia—Spaniards
Englishmen—Maquina's
four wives
and many children—
benches lined with skins
matrix-issue ceremony
King's daughter the princess
bearer to the male heir
Vancouver and Bodega
white chiefs as witness
ceremonial transfer
of would-be rights
entailment-bestowal
diplomacy
protocol (mutual)
European
and 'native'

iii. a feast

Royal kitchen
singing & feast
in a corner
cooks busily employed
Stews & Fricasees
boiling Oil
Porpoise Whale Seal
'such delicious meets
thrown away on us
as it turned out
we had a far better
dinner to sit down to'
agreed on setting out
'Don Quadra
should furnish the eatables

Captn. Vancouver the
Drinkables'

iv. the dance

Maquina loaned his Spanish chain mail
and soldier's helmet
to his brother for the dance
'a complete Suit of Stage Armour
very likely once the property
of Hamlet's Ghost'
the dancers mimed belligerent
people of strange coasts
China England Spain Owyhee
N. W. of Greenwich so remote
wild black eyelash time
bird down and red ochre
clung to fishoiled hairdos
a masque of assault by stealth
a show of bravado 'advancing
with eyes steadily fixed'
down on Indian nation
painted-face warriors brandished
muskets & spears
toward the (unnerved) commanders
stomped swung clubs
drummed gun butts
on the ground in unison
pre-attack chants
and long martial songs
'all fierce & Warlike
style & subject
one or two of them ended
with a frightful yell
to a strangers ear
terrific'

v. potlatch party

party followed—shaman's dance
    'dextrous Pantomimical tricks
    with his Hat & Mask'
pulling strings & changing faces
           a schlepper
came forth now with
    prime skins
      of sea otter
        for the guests—
the king's mouthpiece
speechifying—
Vancouver answered back
   with a fife
      and drum reel—
Maquina ecastatic—
Vancouver promised fireworks—

Isla de   on their way back
Quadra   the relieved captains
y Vancouver   named the island
               after themselves

Erasure of Empire
(Nootka   28 March, 1795)

Spanish flag hauled down ending
last white settlement of the place
closed the fort recalled the garrison sailed
Indians moved in took everything apart
lingering traces a few straggling
turnips and peas in Alberni's garden
Maquina's people let go untouched
ten years till Jewitt stranded ate them
the bones of a few unfortunate
Spaniards in the graveyard—dug up
exhumed by the Indians
to remove the nails from the coffins
for making fish hooks

7
Hard Bargain

adepts

Cleveland of Boston 1799
found Coast Indians could expect
ten Boston ships any given season
set their own skin rates and go
ship to ship with cunning to derive
all possible advantage by ruse of
assertions of offers made to them
which had no foundation in truth
hardly innocents in dealing indeed
as well versed in the tricks of the trade
as the greatest adepts

Words invented since their contact
with White Men   (Sproat, 1868)

Ah-ohpkah-kook, sugar
Ah-wutsetsos, a long dining-table
Choo-chuk, a spoon
Chechamutlpyik, a boat
Chechik, trigger of a gun
Cheetayik, a saw
Chukswih, a waistcoat
Chupox, brass
Eishkook, a bottle
Himmix, lard
Hissits, an axe
Hoh-ha-um, a percussion cap
Hokidskook, a biscuit
Huppah-yukkaik, a brush
Innik-ayik, a stove
Kah-pooh, a coat
Kahchuk, a fork
Kaytshitl, to write
Keitseh-kaytsah, writing
Keitselh, paper, letter, book
Keitsetsos, a writing-table
Klah-klah-pukkah, to hammer a nail
Klah-pukmah, a nail
Kleekqushin, boots
Kleeshklukkaik, trousers
Klyklydskook, bread, flour
Kluk-kaik, a key
Kluppay-uk, scissors
Kokkumyahklassum, a pin

Koquawtselh, a portrait
Koquissuna-pyik, corkscrew
Mookshitl, the hammer of a gun
Mooshussemayik, a hinge
Mootsasook, gunpowder
Mutlsah, to lock (a door)
Oh-puxoonlh, a button
Pah-pahts-uktl, a loaf
Pay-ha-yek, a looking-glass
Pay-pay-huyxm, glass, a window
Quas-setsos, a chair
Sikkah-ik, a frying-pan
Sis-sidskook, rice
Soo-oolh, a kettle
Tah-haytlim, ramrod
Teemel-oomah, a towel
Teena, a file
Too-mees, coal
Tsaykipkaylhool, blacksmith
Wismah, blacking
Yahk-pus, a bearded man
Zah-wha, a wheel
Zoktââs, a cart

riches

                        Run-of-the-mill
industrial revolution manufactured goods
superfluous blankets and dinged-up copper tea kettles
                        in a country without tea
a necklace of old keys polished by so much touching
prestige comes from status goods 'Indian wealth'
conferring rank by way of display privileges
At Nootka Gray was charged a six inch
scrap of sheet copper (and thought it costly)
for a two feet by five jet black thick
                        short glossy
'prime' skin   'They do not seem to covet
usefull things' noted the *Columbia*'s supercargo
Hoskins, in charge of the business end,
'but anything that looks pleasing
to the eye, or what they call riches'

Bargaining   (Sproat, 1868)

'Commodities are obtained among the Ahts from one another by bartering slaves, canoes, and articles of food, clothing, or ornament; and from the colonists by exchanging oil, fish, skins, and furs. All the natives are acute, and rather too sharp at bargaining. The Ahts are fond of a long conversation in selling, but seldom reduce their price; living at no expense, they can afford to keep their stock of goods a long time on hand. I have known an Indian keep a sea-otter's skin more than three years, though repeatedly offered a fair price for it.'

Inflation (collusion = extermination)

Skin currency and exchange rates
always an unconscious
collusion for extermination sharp

price hike early 1790s skin
prices climbing up and down the Coast
Indians now have plenty of iron for tools

want display items copper blankets
interchangeable media for
potlatching Indian 'money' *muskets*

demanded more and more for skins
as killing instruments in hunting
as well as war removing

the metaphor the sea
otters can now be killed by Indians directly
not only for but *by* the *money*

Price Controls   (Sproat, 1868)

'News about prices, and indeed about anything in which the natives take an interest, travels quickly to distant places from one tribe to another. If a trading schooner appeared at one point on the shore, and offered higher prices than one usually given, the Indians would know the fact immediately along the whole coast. The coasting intertribal trade is not free, but is arbitrarily controlled by the stronger tribes, who will not allow weaker tribes to go past them in search of customers; just as if the people of Hull should intercept all vessels laden with cargo from the north of England for London, and make the people of London pay for them an exaggerated price, fixed by the interceptors.'

inland business

Maquina
dealt overland
in skins
with the Nimpkish

Wickaninish too
with backwoods people
who still wanted iron
bringing in

inside passage goods
to deal at outside
summer villages
superseding fishing

would have
induced total
starvation
if not for 'prestige goods'

skin business based on give and take

Dealing begins with chanting
leading to extensive quibbling

The quality of merchandise
is ritually distorted

Patience threshold limits
the opportunistic trader

Who can't stand and wait
hour after hour to listen

Business with Indians
begins and ends with singing

Exchange of goods
is passed off as gift giving

Purchases disguised as gifts
come dearest of all

Protocol is cultural
but business is still business

After each transaction
there is further song and dance

the system of exchange

Marchand
'It is the usage of the natives to terminate no bargain
without demanding a present, which they call *stok*.
On voit que déjà ils commencent à s'*européaniser*.'

Sturgis
'Several smaller articles were given as presents
nominally, but in reality formed part of the price.'

Sturgis disdained haggling for hours
with a woman over a piece of thread
        he said

Wickaninish's Revenge   (1811)

A few days
after Capt. Thorne
intemperate commander
of Astor's *Tonquin*
pushed the face
of the Indian in
the profferred skin
(the price
displeased him)
reciprocation
was insisted upon
the Indians
bashed in Capt. Thorne's
hot blooded brain pan
with a *pautumaugan*

after the surprise attack

Lewis the clerk was down in the hold hiding
bleeding to death
he lit the powder magazine
took the last
breath taken on the *Tonquin*
by a white man bringing
at least four Indians
to the watery underworld with him
Yankee-trader wreckage scattered all over the Sound
including some trading blankets woven in New York
factories
which scavenged from the junk-charged waters
became significant display privilege
items among the Indians
known as 'Clayoquot blankets'
for many potlatch seasons to come

order of business in trade

> haranguing   feasting
> singing   dancing
> gift giving   haranguing
> feasting
> singing   dancing
>
> sleeping—
> or the taking of the ship

artificial starvation

In Macao Capts. King & Gore
sold sixpenny Nootkan cutsarks
for 100 Spanish gold dollars

Chinese mandarins prized
dark brown furs from
cold northern waters

acquisition and prestige
hand-in-hand motives
everything changed Nootkans

turned from the old seasonal
hunt storing up dog
salmon from the fall run

and January herring
to chase after sea otter
satisfy some chief's hunger

for wealth goods—you
can't eat hammered copper
a long winter in the downpour

walking the beaches
picking through drift kelp for
storm-killed pilchard

or a codfish head
left behind as
seal or sea lion garbage

late

'In the midst of abundance'
Indians dying of starvation
sitting around idle between local wars
abandoning fishing for wealth goods
no more otters left   no ships
the vicissitude of the trade
18th century adventuring ending

8
Captive

acquisition and innocence

'The idea of a "traditional" order is misleading. For there is no innocence in the established proprietors, at any particular point in time, unless we ourselves choose to put it there. Very few titles to property could bear humane investigation, in the long process of conquest.'

—Raymond Williams,
The Country and the City

'Rights obtained by conquest were regarded as "having a bad name," i.e. not so noble as those obtained by inheritance or marriage. Captured rights were called *tcinōkt*... In quarrels a man will say, "Those rights you claim are not good, they are something stolen. They are just *tcinōkt*." His opponent can make no reply, even if it was his ancestors way back who got them in war.'

—Philip Drucker,
The Northern and Central Nootkan Tribes

the ship Boston

The *Boston* sailed round
the Horn to Nootka

and anchored
five miles above Friendly Cove

in a spot where Capt. Salter
hoped to find wood and water

to sustain the ship in that shelter
while skins were got by trade

Business was to be done
with the great king of the Nootkans

Maquina regal in knee length
cutsark jet black white fringed

red paint a glossy patina
covering copper dark skin

crescent moons mascara'd
above dark eyes that shone over

Roman nose sagacious
imperial forehead

long black oil-saturated mane
sprinkled with white eagle's down

the sun chief

Maquina the whale hunter   *tsaxhw'sip*
conqueror of nations   the harpooner
eater of babies   grew fond of tea
replaced his cutsark
          with pantaloons

donned a steel helmet
     and Iberian mail

     (chief's religious role)

      Ma kwee na
        'chief of the sun'

        king of the whole
        black silver gold
        oracle sky

His rituals   VISIONS
periodic hungers   produced
self-deprivations   PROPHECY

he locked himself for days
in a wooden box
painted inside with fetishes

went into a trance
commenced to rave
outside the box his relatives convened
          taking notes

The Taking of the Boston   *(22 March, 1803)*

Chief Maquina
fell out with Capt. Salter
over that common thing
the Captain's loan of a gun
which the Chief brought back
with one busted flint lock
called it *peshak* (bad)
Salter swung
the double barreled shotgun
at the Indian's head
the stock broke
Maquina with a bump
on his head
got back in his canoe
went off in a huff
and did not come back
on board till four days
had passed
when with some chiefs
and many braves
he showed up
war-painted
in a bear mask
danced
and sang in apparent
conciliatory manner

Salter took him back aboard
they dined in the Captain's cabin
the Chief

in friendly fashion
offered a tip
on a salmon run
the Captain
sent off several men
in a pinnace to fish when
the pinnace had gone off
several braves
pretending to offer a hand
in hoisting off a second boat
threw Capt. Salter overboard
alongside the ship
there was a canoe
with some Indian women in it
they pulled out clubs
and bashed in the Captain's skull
as he flailed in the water

On deck the gang of warriors
drew concealed weapons
and finished off the crew
decapitating them
all save the sailmaker Thompson
and the metal worker Jewitt scalped
whose terrible salvation
began with
the forced inspection on deck
of the row of twenty-five heads

retentive

The sowing of the dragon's teeth

Maquina listed for Jewitt
    the crimes of Martínez
    Hanna and the rest

They resolved to kill the first
    outsider who came into their territory
    whoever that might be

This was *tcitcmo*

Company for the dead

The first arrivals are always
    unsuspecting
    set upon without warning
    attacked and slain

Vindictiveness   (Sproat, 1868)

'The Aht natives are very revengeful, and appear to cherish rancour for a length of time, sometimes for more than one generation. Disputes between individuals lead to implacable family feuds. Though it is usual to accept large presents as expiation for murder, yet, practically, this expiation is not complete, and blood alone effectually atones for blood. An accepted present never quite cancels the obligation to punish in the breast of the offended person or tribe. Many years after the offence, and, generally when disappointed in some blood-thirsty expedition, these savages will call to mind an old injury, and make it the pretext for a murderous attack on an unsuspecting tribe.'

how much you have to put up with
        to get copper
        to potlatch with

To ignore an insult is to lose face (rank status)
humiliation is worse than bodily injury
people seeing you seeming to be brought low *is* being brought
                                                        low
ergo absolute sensitivity a necessity
your rank status demands it
(outsiders don't understand this)

loot

The Indians rifled the ship *Boston*
dressed up in women's clothing smocks & sacks
pulled high stocking caps over their heads
draped their necks
with powder horns & bags of shot
came from all around to party four days
till two Boston ships came into the Sound to trade
the *Juno* and the *Mary*
the Indians scared them off with great
whooping and shooting of guns
signalling no trade

after the taking of the ship

fifty chemises

scattered on the beach

an 8 powder horn necklace
worn
by an inferior chief

in a woman's stocking
cap

a victory
feast————but

the second temple was not like the first
the chief uttered in the nightmare
words *divide, inclose, oppose, rent*

to show the hunters the way

the otter sprang ahead of them
its own swimming presentness

woke up a slave

John Jewitt a young armourer embarked from Hull
whose father a blacksmith
built a forge for him on deck
on which he might pound out hatchets
and knives for the Indian trade and maintain
the three thousand muskets in the cargo hold

lights out   woke up a slave

Maquina ordered him spared
to work metals
                make warriors' knives
                    bracelets for his wives
and to keep his
three thousand new muskets clean

a partner in exile

March 22, 1803

Chief told me I must get ship under way   take her into the Cove   we arrived at 8 o'clock in the evening   Chief took me ashore   I slept at his house   as soon as I arrived in the house natives came around me   seemed to sympathize in my captivity   I was very uneasy   in a great deal of pain   laid myself down to go to sleep   alarmed about 12 o'clock by natives coming into the house   told me one of our people still alive   I rejoiced reflecting I should be much more happy having a partner in exile   immediately went on board   to my great joy found our Sailmaker Thompson   he had received a stab in the nose Chief expressed great satisfaction in his being saved   saying he would be very useful to make sails for his canoes

salvage

before the ship *Boston*
    could be stripped
      of all her cargo
an Indian
    coming aboard one night
      to pilfer
set her afire with a torch
    and burned her
      to the water

Jewitt found a blank book
    in the Captain's cabin
      before the *Boston* burned
kept a journal of his captivity
    written in blackberry juice
      covertly

business was poor

By Jewitt's time business was poor for Maquina
the Chief had scoured the Coast for skins
even overland from the backward Nimpkish
but when no ships came in range of his guns
to trade with him two long lean seasons
started to seem easier just to pick the plum
of representation that was the *Boston*
a ship representing *giving* by *taking*

sinking the owning boat

Maquina the ship bandit
stole to give away his booty
but the ship sank—like
a canoe with a leak

the chief put there
by chopping a hole in it
with a hatchet sinks
to the bottom of the Sound

sinking the owning boat
as a form of giving it away
destruction of property
shows a strong and willing heart

the rune of acquisition hidden
within the stave of
the hatchet   the blanket   the canoe
at the bottom of the Sound

during Jewitt's captivity

November 1, 1803
> Heavy rains herald the dark month of November
> a canoe from the Clayoquots arrives   Wickani-
> nish the visitors relate has recently conducted a
> successful campaign against an enemy tribe
> claimed 150 men and women as his victims
> nine slaves acquired in that contest have been
> brought along as gifts of Wickaninish to Maquina
> in return Maquina sends back to his fellow native
> generalissimo canoes laden with cloth muskets
> powder and shot and other precious articles taken
> from the cargo hold of the Boston

Slavery   (Sproat, 1868)

'No institution is more specifically defined among
the Ahts than that of slavery. It has probably existed
in these tribes for a long time, as many of the slaves
have a characteristic mean expression, and the word
"slave" is used commonly as a term of reproach. If a
man acts meanly or is niggardly in his distributions
of property, it is said that he has a "slave's heart."
Next to a "heart of water," which means a coward,
the "heart of a slave" is the most opprobrious
epithet.   Formerly almost every well-born native
owned a slave, and some of the chiefs had five or
six. A slave was considered a useful and honourable
possession, and if sold or lost, was replaced imme-
diately by another. The slave is at the absolute
disposal of his master in all things; he is a bond-
servant who may be transferred without his own
consent from one proprietor to another. So complete
is the power over slaves, and the indifference to
human life among the Ahts, that an owner might
bring half a dozen slaves out of his house and kill
them publicly in a row without any notice being
taken of the atrocity.'

208

Maquina liked a good clean cut

Maquina liked a good clean cut
one of war's fine arts, a neat well-executed beheading

the captive sailmaker Thompson was a navy man
grizzled veteran of the glory days with Lord Howe

'perfectly fearless' 'wholly regardless of his life'
always kept his cutlass with him, and *sharp*

one day was out doing slave's duties
washing the chief's blanket humiliated grumbling

a low rank fellow visiting from up the Coast
tromped on the blanket with dirty feet

looked Thompson in the eye and laughed
Thompson cut off the fellow's head for that

rolled it up in the blanket and brought it to the chief
Jewitt reports 'the king was much pleased'

the armourer's dream

Far aft, the officers peered watchfully to windward through the mist of squalls. Water tumbled in cataracts over the forecastle doors. The tin oil-lamp suspended on a long string, smoking, described wide circles; wet clothing made dark heaps on the glistening floor. In the bed-places men lay booted, resting on elbows and with open eyes. Then came the image that always awakened Jewitt from the recurring dream. Hung-up suits of oil skin swung out and in, lively and disquieting like reckless ghosts of decapitated seamen dancing in a tempest.

frustrations of the hunt

April 5, 1804

    Chief went out whaling   first time this season
no success

April 6, 1804

    Thick and cloudy   chief out whaling   struck one
was fast but harpoon broke   he lost him   re-
turned very cross

April 15, 1805

    Chief out whaling   struck two but his harpoon
drawed   returned in very bad humor

Maquina's whale hunt scorecard
during Jewitt's captivity

Days the chief went whaling	53
whales struck and lost	8
whales killed	1

whaling season seems
everybody went hungry

third moon

Third moon   deep winter time   food resources
                           getting slim
Gift privileges for coming parties greatly
occupy ranking minds
                whose 'catch' is it?

        'the harpooner'
        tsaxhw'sip

wears an image
    of a great whale hunter
on his woven yellow cedar conical
    hat

hungry

March 30, 1803

    Rummaging in the wreck   found a box of
chocolate   much delighted   having for some
time nothing to eat but whale's blubber and train
oil

June 9, 1803

    Walked from house to house begging for
something to eat   cockles   we accepted

June 18, 1803

    Nothing to eat all day

July 7, 1803

    Nothing to eat for two days but nettle stalks

Spanish introduction
of vegetable gardens
at Friendly Cove
went unattended
and unconsumed ten seasons
till Thompson and Jewitt
ate all the peas
in one sitting

Jewitt's lake

June 12, 1803

      Washed   put on clean shirts   went out amongst
      bushes with prayerbook   pray to God to send a
      ship

      Under the starcrowded night
      skies tremolo bird
      calls echoing in cedars

      the quiet eyes of the lake
      where Jewitt went to bathe
      and pray for his release

      are shining shining cool
      and wet with distance
      and silent lamentation

a cautionary tale

October 24, 1803

Our Chief informed me that not long ago there were six men ran away in the night on account of bad treatment from the captain and for being kept on short allowance from the ship Manchester of Philadelphia when she lay at Nootka   he gave me a book belonging to one of the men that ran away named Daniel Smith and I found by looking into it that the other men's names were Lewis Gillion James   Toms   Benjamin Johnson   Jack Clark was informed by our Chief that six of them went away in the night unknown to him expecting to get to the Wickeninishes but being very hungry were obliged to stop at the Esquates several miles this side of their intended port   natives stopt them from going any further knowing they belonged to our Chief and brought them back to Nootka   he was very angry   ordered them to be killed which the natives did   the ship's boy Jack did not run away so his life was spared and sold to Wickeninishes   soon after we arrived he heard of our ship's being cut off   he died in May 1803

seasonal festivities

December 13, 1803

Our Chief began a most curious farce   all the chiefs were invited to a feast   all of a sudden the Chief fired a pistol close against his son's ear frightened them all   natives running up and down the village pulling hair out from their heads by handfulls   crying out our Chief's son is dead   all of a sudden came into the house two men dressed in wolves' skins   took the child away on their backs   we were ordered out of the house for seven days   if we came within that time he said he would kill us   after seven days he called for us to come to the house

December 21, 1803

The farce ended with a horrible sight   three of the natives pierced through the flesh of each side near to the ribs with a bayonet   play performed every year in the month of December

December 24, 1803

Employed making daggers   eighteen inches long polished so as to see one's face in them

December 25, 1803

Christmas day   bought our suppers   dried clams and train oil   employed as usual

December 25, 1804

Employed washing our garment which is a fathom

of blue cloth   suffer greatly from cold weather having only this small garment to cover our nakedness

December 26, 1804
Frosty weather   Christmas time in my native country but a sorrowful time for me   employed cutting firewood

elder moon ritual

                                     if primogeniture
              hadn't vanished in thin air
                a handsome signory   greets the son

     Ma Kwee na   elder moon
                                         potlatch season
              all over the Sound
                        it's midnight

                                         rights to certain
              songs & dances   streams & names
                masks   seines & traps

                such profligacy of estate

        to police the farce
                  supernatural wolves waltz in
        (you can hear every black star)
                        make off with the children

     (novices) 'kidnapped'   confusion

                    Yuquot = swept by wind

at Maquina's wolf dance

because the lake
    he bathed in
        was *his*
the lake people
    danced
        the lake
people dance—
        they painted their
            faces white
with big black
    popeye circles
        big wide frog mouths
they stuffed
    blankets from
        the ship in
their clothes
    big fat frog bellies

they hopped into
    the house
        and
croaked and
    hopped
        around

the house

New Year's hopes

January 21, 1804

> Arrived a canoe from northward to inform our Chief there were twenty-five ships coming to Nootka to destroy his tribe caused him to look very shy upon us

January 22, 1804

> Now began to be downhearted our Chief said he would cut off another ship if he possibly could I hope God will prevent him

January 23, 1804

> Rainy all the native discourse is to cut off another ship if one arrives

January 24, 1804

> Arrived a canoe from same tribe eight natives brought the same news respecting ships frightened us very much

January 25, 1804

> Frosty weather left Cooptee to return to Nootka about twenty miles distance arrived at Nootka P.M. having had hard work and nothing to eat

January 26, 1804
Sunday Employed making our houses two canoes from Wickeninishes prayers as usual

January 27, 1804
>Fine and clear   entertained hopes of seeing a
ship in the course of two months

disheartened

March 22, 1804

Begin to look for ships every day hoping for our release as soon as one shall arrive   sufferings amongst these savages incredible   they are the most filthy people in the world   eating the vermin of their own bodies while cooking their meals   we are very much disheartened

May 21, 1804

This day I am twenty-one years of age   I now begin to give up all hopes of ever seeing a Christian country or a Christian face   the season being so far advanced and not hearing of the arrival of any ship on the coast   we feel ourselves very unhappy

July 30, 1804

Very much disheartened to think we frequently hear of ships arriving on the coast and that none will come off Nootka to enable us to communicate with them

January 28, 1805
Sunday   Much dejected at hearing of ships on the coast and that not one of them attempt to release us

matchmaking

July 31, 1804

    Chief meeting with other chiefs of tribe to determine whether he should give me a wife   thinking it would be better for me than to live single   said it was very uncertain when any ship would come to our release

September 10, 1804

    This day our Chief bought a wife for me   told me I must not refuse her   if I did he would have both Thompson and myself killed   custom of natives on being married is that the man and his wife must not sleep together for ten nights immediately succeeding marriage   very much against my inclination to take one of these heathens for a partner but will be for my advantage while I am amongst them for she has a father who always goes fishing   I shall live much better than I have heretofore

March 21, 1805

    Very sick and downhearted   Chief gave me liberty to dispense with the girl he had forced me to take for a partner which I did with great satisfaction

old scores forgotten

Jewitt took a wife
adopted Indian costume
got sick from exposure
divorced his Indian wife
put back on his ragged
white world clothing

two years passed
one day in 1805
was at his stone anvil
heating up a dagger
on his homemade forge
when the ship *Lydia* appeared

Captain Samuel Hill commander
invited Maquina aboard
slapped him in irons
would have shot him
but for the intercession
of the forgiving armourer

An old Indian told... *(Sproat, 1868)*

'An old Indian told the late W. E. Banfield, a well-known trader on the coast, that he had been a youthful servitor in the family of the chief Klan-nin-ittle during the bondage of Jewitt and Thompson, and that he often assisted Jewitt in carrying the bows, arrows and other weapons which Klan-nin-ittle used in hostile expeditions. He said further that the white slave generally accompanied his owner on visits of courtesy, which in quiet times he frequently paid to the tribes of Ayhuttisaht, Ahousaht, and Klah-oh-quat. Jewitt, it seems, was a general favourite, owing to his good-humour and light-heartedness; and he often recited and sang in his own language for the amusement of the savages. He was described as a tall, well-made youth, with a mirthful countenance, whose dress, latterly, consisted of nothing but a mantle of cedar-bark. There was a long story also of Jewitt's courting, and, I think, finally abducting the charming daughter of the Ahousaht chief, Waugh-clagh; with which, however, I shall not trouble the reader.'

The Captive Liberated

i.

Jewitt was a child of time
   not so far removed from days
      when everything was from the hand of God

went out into Empire
   when in his first weeks upon the sea
      immensity inseparable companion of a ship's life

pressed down upon him
   he had no trouble understanding
      what kept him one moment to the next

from a watery termination
   not that thin skin
      of planks and copper

separating him from the ocean
   but the hand of Providence
      in whose palm he and everybody rode

ii.

Captivity   hardship
   cold   hunger
      humiliation   fear

his trust in Providence
   in his own fate
      which allowed him to endure

the horror
    by 'going
        wild' afterwards

prevented his returning
    to 'civilized' ways
        so that

the unwilling child
    of nature first
        captive then a slave

later adoptive son
    finally the betrayer
        of the grand sun king

watched stars showering
    through northern lights
        like grindstone sparks

thrown off the fiery wheel
    behind his eyes
        as the skies darkening

closed off from him
    his former understanding
        of a European life

iii.

The captive liberated yet
    would never again be able
        any more than squeeze

himself back into the frock
    coat of his school boy days
        put back on the trust

of the cheerful enlightened
   child had sustained him
      in his uneasy exodus

into nature
   two years plotting escape
      pleas for aid desperate reached

the captain who brought ship in
   to rescue him
      he met the vehicle of his salvation

with face painted
   crazy hair dressed after
      the fashion of the savages

from whom he was putatively being saved

         iv.

For a few dollars more
   was persuaded
      to adopt if not adapt

to publish the journal of his soul
   with the hand
      of a Connecticut Defoe

guiding his own
   evolved a narrative
      of his adventures

out of the behavior
   of those demons now drove him
      to wander 'unsettled

in his habits'   with small joy
 peddling his book
  New York Salem Boston

in a horse drawn cart
 when the horse broke down
  employed a wheelbarrow

with a playwright's help
 transfigured again
  those events in Indian nation

to a stage farce
 ending in pathos
  the captive

liberated
 singing 'The Song
  of the Armourer's Boy'

  v.

abject at last lapsed
 back into wildness
  donned the customs

of his Indian
 captors   devastated
  corrupted by White Word

white world ways drank
 abandoned American
  wife and children

trailed forlorn
 through summer resorts
  in the Pennsylvania

hills   a few dollars more
    performing 'Nootka
        Songs in Nootka Costume'

fell away from 'foolish conceits'
    the religion of his fathers
        among playgoers

died
    shattered age 38
        in Hartford

zeitgeist

time ghost in a skin cloak walking
the chromosomes don't lie
forty to seventy
thousand years ago
ancestors of Wickaninish and Maquina
trekked down from Kamchatka
      over the land bridge
      in the 'dawn of time'

a blink of the eye
to a sea otter   back-floating
cracking open a mussel
with a piece of abalone shell

      Spanish English
Boston men sailed in
on a wind from the future
      late last night
      to get skins
were gone by morning

empire of skin

The impress of empire in a flipping coin
A chance impression—empire of the skin—
The act of representation itself
Has its own powers of implication.
Becoming once more a still, plane surface
After having engulfed a person, life goes on
Without even a ripple at the vanishing point,
And from that life that person's excluded,
As will, as knowledge, as any other thing
Except a memory, growing dim,
The way a sentence left uncompleted
Appears to sink deeper into the paper,
As the coin falls toward tabulated
Foliate columns, a flat unscrolling moon.

Printed October 1997 in Santa Barbara
& Ann Arbor for the Black Sparrow Press by
Mackintosh Typography & Edwards Brothers Inc.
Text set in Korinna by Words Worth.
Design by Barbara Martin.
This first edition is published in paper wrappers;
there are 200 hardcover trade copies;
100 hardcover copies have been numbered &
signed by the author; & 20 signed copies lettered
A–T have been handbound in boards by Earle Gray,
each with an original drawing by Tom Clark.

PRINTER'S COPY

Tom Clark

Photo: Chris Felver

Poet, historian, novelist, critic and biographer, Tom Clark was born (1941) and raised on the West Side of Chicago. He attended the Universities of Michigan (B.A.) and Cambridge (M.A.), and has worked variously as editor, writer and teacher. Though associated since the 1960s with the New York School of poets, for much of the past thirty years he has made his home in California—since 1984 in Berkeley. His writing of recent years has often engaged in explorations of lost worlds; or as the critic Alva Svoboda has put it (speaking of *Like Real People*), "the mysterious way in which 'lost time' can be both gone and present, and the inhabitants of that time (including the poet himself) both real and like real people."